THE FUTURE OF THE KINGDOM
IN PROPHECY AND FULFILLMENT

THE FUTURE OF THE KINGDOM IN PROPHECY AND FULFILLMENT

*A Study of the Scope of
"Spiritualization" in Scripture*

BY

MARTIN J. WYNGAARDEN, A.M., B.D., Ph.D.

*Professor of Old Testament Interpretation
Calvin Theological Seminary, Grand Rapids, Mich.
Sometime Fellow at Pennsylvania and at Yale
and Scholar at Princeton Seminary; Member
of The American Oriental Society; The
Chicago Society of Biblical Research
and The Society of Biblical
Literature and Exegesis*

WIPF & STOCK · Eugene, Oregon

Wipf and Stock Publishers
199 W 8th Ave, Suite 3
Eugene, OR 97401

The Future of the Kingdom in Prophecy and Fulfillment
A Study of the Scope of "Spiritualization" in Scripture
By Wyngaarden, Martin J.
ISBN 13: 978-1-60608-029-0
Publication date 1/13/2011
Previously published by Baker Book House, 1955

In appreciation of my early teachers
  Geerhardus Vos and R. D. Wilson
  J. A. Montgomery and A. T. Clay

PREFACE

Much interest is displayed in prophecies and their fulfillment. But their study gives rise to a leading question. Which prophecies must be understood literally and which spiritually?

In other words, what is the scope, the realm, the sphere of spiritualization in the Scriptures, as evidenced by the Word of God? This is the main problem here under consideration, especially in chapters I, VIII and X.

Chapter I is reprinted from *The Banner* by permission. Various requests followed its publication, for a continuation of the discussion. Here then is the continuation, with materials that had been gradually developed in certain courses, as the background for the interpretation of the preaching of the prophets.

To the literature on the subject, the writer is deeply indebted, though his greatest obligation is to the concordances and lexicons, in order that the Biblical evidence, itself, might be explored and adduced.

For relatively few works were found that treat the *scope* of the kind of prophecy that is spiritually interpreted, by the Scriptures, — in contrast with the *scope* of the many literally fulfilled prophecies.

The present attempt to search out the Biblical evidence that may be adduced, in connection with this problem, may, therefore, hopefully, be of use. This evidence is presented especially in chapter VIII, and discussed in chapter X.

Some consideration is also given to the predicted Jewish return to the ancient Holy Land, — after the exile, not only. But attention is also given to the growing Jewish colonies in Palestine, today, some of which were visited, by the author, in 1931; and some inquiry is made into the related theme of a possible literal fulfillment of prophecy, in connection with the Jewish return to Palestine, in our times.

PREFACE

Some of the esteemed readers may possibly recall that it was the writer's privilege to read the substance of chapters VII, VIII and X, before The Chicago Society of Biblical Research, on different occasions; and part of chapter V before The American Oriental Society.

This little book is humbly inscribed in appreciation of some of his early teachers and guides, two still living. Guides to Biblical research they were, all.

But the writer's greatest debt he owes to that most modest of scholars, Dr. Geerhardus Vos, formerly professor of Biblical Theology at Princeton, whose courses were an incentive for the present work. During a number of years, that incentive has accumulated, as its fruit, the present contribution, on the eschatology of the theocracy, — the future of the typical Kingdom of God.

Evidence is adduced for the spiritualization of the entire typical kingdom, including the vital elements Israel, Zion, and the Promised Land, — fundamental either to the millennium or to our final glory.

May this Biblical evidence contribute, therefore, to illumine Israel's significance, in connection with Christ's Church.

But may these studies be used, chiefly, to magnify the glorified Christ, the Righteous Servant to Jehovah — Isaiah 53:11.

Finally, this little work is sent forth with the prayer that it may prove valuable in interpreting the Biblical approach to Christmas, Easter, Ascension Day and Pentecost; and useful in understanding the predictive approach to Christ's Second Coming, — according to the glorious prophecies of our covenant God.

Calvin Seminary, M. J. W.
Grand Rapids, Mich.
February 20, 1934.

TABLE OF CONTENTS

CHAPTER	PAGE
PREFACE	7

I. WONDERS OF JEHOVAH'S PROPHECY 13
Were Any O. T. Prophecies Fulfilled Literally?
Fulfilled Prophecies concerning:
- A. The Mighty Tyre: Predicted to be Destroyed — 14
- B. Sidon Abiding: The Predicted Bloodshed.... — 17
- C. Judgments Forecast for Samaria — 19
- D. Zion to be Plowed as a Field — 20

II. THE CHALLENGE 23
"In principle a scientific Calvinistic hermeneutics looks with distrust upon . . . spiritualizing".... 23
"It is just the Calvinist who blows hot and cold at the same time, when he sublimates these plain declarations favoring Chiliasm into the dust clouds of a forced exegesis" 25
Requirement: The *Biblical Evidence* for the Spiritualizing Objected to by Premillenarians; Reference to Chapters VIII and IX 25

III. "A KINGDOM OF PRIESTS AND A HOLY NATION," Ex. 19:6; I Peter 2:9 26
Concession: Many prophecies were literally fulfilled: Survey 26
Yet there is a future of the typical kingdom, in prophecy and fulfillment, that involves the spiritualization evidenced in Chapters VIII and IX 27–28
THE CHARACTER OF THIS TYPICAL KINGDOM 28
- A. Formal Establishment of the Typical Kingdom — 28
- B. The Rule of the Typical Kingdom — 29
- C. Human Agencies Provided for Israel to Carry out Jehovah's Will — 31
- D. Critical View of the Theocracy — 33
- E. The End of the Theocracy — 35

IV. PROPHETIC TYPES OF CHRIST AND OF HIS CHURCH 37
The Future of the Typical Kingdom is Mirrored Prominently, *First, in History*, in the Prophecies Touching the Prophetic Types 38
- A. Moses and His Prophetic Eschatological Significance — 39

CHAPTER		PAGE
	B. The Angel of Jehovah and His Eschatological Meaning	40
	C. The Royal Prophet and His Eschatological Import	41
	D. The Eschatological Servant of Jehovah, in Isaiah, Performs Prophetic Work	43
	E. The Eschatology of the Prophetic Office Involves not only the Individual Prophet, but also the Collective Body of the Faithful	45
V.	ROYAL TYPES OF CHRIST AND OF HIS CHURCH	47
	The Future of the Kingdom is Heralded in Prophecies touching especially the Royal Types, somewhat *Later in History*	47
	A. Earlier Kings and their Typical Import	47
	B. Later Kings and their Prophetic Significance	48
	C. The Royal Servant of Jehovah in Isaiah and His Messianic Import	49
	a. Identification of the Royal Messiah with the Suffering Servant of Jehovah	49
	b. Citation of O. T. Materials Lending Support to this Identification	50
	D. Concluding Royal Messianic Prophecies	55
VI.	PRIESTLY AND SACRIFICIAL TYPES OF CHRIST AND OF HIS CHURCH	57
	The Future of the Kingdom is Foreshadowed in Prophecies touching especially the Priestly Types, these Prophecies of Jehovah Coming Chiefly, *still Later in History*	57
	A. Identification of the Priestly and the Kingly Figure in Prophecy	57
	B. Eschatological Prophecies concerning the Priesthood and its Typical Importance	59
	C. Prophecies concerning the Sacrifices and their Future Significance	62
	D. Prophecies concerning the Temple and its Eschatological Meaning	66
VII.	WILL THESE O. T. TYPES BE FULFILLED IN PREMILLENNIAL FASHION?	70
	A. Presentation of the Premillennial Principles of Interpretation	70
	B. Import and Criticism of the Premillennial Interpretations	71
	C. Conclusions as to the Contradictory Interpretations Thus Arising	75
	D. Transition to the Study of the Evidence for Determining the Biblical Scope of Spiritualization	80

CHAPTER	PAGE
VIII. HOW THEN WOULD CHRIST BECOME KING OF JERUSALEM?	83

If not Premillennially, How Then? He would become king, according to the prophecies, as these are interpreted in harmony with the spiritual interpretations indicated by the Scriptures ... 83

I. Meaning of Spiritual Interpretation Applying to Jerusalem and to the Other Elements Connected with the Typical Kingdom ... 84

II. Presentation of the Evidence that the Scriptures Interpret Spiritually Jerusalem, the Promised Land, Israel, even all the Abiding Features Connected with the Typical O. T. Kingdom that Reappear in Christ's Kingdom ... 87

   A. There is a Latency of Spiritualization in the O. T. and an Evident Spiritualization in the N. T. of the Permanent Elements Connected with the Typical Kingdom that Recur in the Kingdom of the Son of God (Col. 1:13) *Spiritualization of*:

      1. Zion and Jerusalem ... 88
      2. The Holy Land as the Inheritance of the Covenant People ... 91
      3. The Kingdom ... 94
      4. The Seed of Abraham, as the Covenant People, Heirs of the Kingdom ... 97
      5. The Covenant People, as the Bride of the Lord ... 98
      6. Israel, the Covenant People, Recipients of the Kingdom ... 100
      7. Israel's Enemies, for Example the Edomites ... 108
      8. The Cultus or Sacrificial System, . . . Ark, . . . Temple, . . . Sacrifices ... 113
      9. Priestly, Royal and Prophetic Types ... 116
      10. The Covenant of Grace, including the Contrast of the "New Covenant" with the Old Covenant ... 121
      11. The O. T. Sacraments, . . . Circumcision, Passover ... 134

   B. There is Especially an Organic Spiritualization of O. T. Scripture ... 135
      1. The Psalter as the Praise-book of the Kingdom ... 136
      2. The O. T. Scriptures as they Treat of the Future of the Kingdom ... 140

   C. Interpretive Principles thus Derived from the Scriptures ... 142

CHAPTER	PAGE
D. How Then Would Christ Become King?....	144
1. Of Jerusalem	144
2. Of the Promised Land	147
3. Over Israel	150

IX. HOW DID CHRIST BECOME KING OF JERUSALEM? 159

Can the prophecies of Christ's Messianic Kingship over Zion be interpreted in the light of any recorded fulfillments in the New Testament?........ 159

The Future of the Typical Kingdom, in the Light of the N. T. Fulfillments Dealing with Christ's Eternal Kingship over His Spiritual Jerusalem, as illumined by his Prophetic Message and as the Reward of His Priestly Work..................... 162

A. The Prophetic Office and the N. T. Fulfillment of the Great Mosaic Prophecy Relating to it.... 162

B. The Priestly Office in the O. T. Prophecies that have Explicit N. T. Fulfillments or Allusions.... 164

C. The Royal Office in O. T. Prophecies having Explicit N. T. Fulfillments or Allusions............ 166

X. THE BIBLICAL SCOPE OF SPIRITUALLY INTERPRETED PROPHECY AND OF LITERAL FULFILLMENTS 173

A. Survey of the Scope of Spiritualization in Scripture, involving the Organic Unity of the Typical Kingdom, as this Kingdom finds its Fulfillment in the Church........................... 174

B. How Apply the Scriptural Guidance thus Given, to Teach us whether a Prophecy was Evidently Intended Literally, or whether it Involved the Spiritual Interpretation of One or More Items 175
   1. The First Question... 175
   2. The Second Question... 176
   3. Application to Prophecies and to Other Biblical Passages 178
   4. The Jewish Return to Palestine as a Literal Fulfillment? 182
   5. Unfulfilled Prophecies 190
   6. Conclusions 192

SUPPLEMENT

Bibliographical Note
Index of Topics
Index of Scripture References

CHAPTER I
WONDERS OF JEHOVAH'S PROPHECY

Were Any Old Testament Prophecies Fulfilled Literally?

Few things can so stimulate one's faith in the revelation of God, as the fulfillments of prophecy. Here we have, first of all, those fulfilled in Christ's ministry, in his sacrifice and resurrection.

But there are also many others fulfilled in the history of great cities and mighty nations, in a most remarkable manner. The fulfillments are so precise, unmistakable, important, and far-reaching as to recall the words of Isaiah, addressed to those inclined to reject Jehovah's predictions: "Produce your cause, saith Jehovah; bring forth your strong reasons, saith the King of Jacob. Let them bring forth, and declare unto us what shall happen: declare ye the former things, what they are, that we may consider them, and know the latter end of them; or show us things to come" (Isa. 41: 21, 22).

To "know the latter end" of Israel and its neighbors means to know their future, their eschatology. For eschatology deals with that group of predictions that tells of things seen by the prophets on the distantly future, prophetic horizon. Anything, therefore, that has to do with the latter days, or the day of Jehovah, or the latter end of things is eschatological, from the Old Testament point of view, irrespective of the time of the fulfillment of the prophecy.

And then we find many[1] literal fulfillments of prophecy, in connection with Israel, as the theocratic nation, and in connection with the surrounding nations referred to by the prophets serving under the theocracy, — the Old Testament kingdom of Jehovah.

Now the very remarkable thing is that those fulfillments are so exceedingly literal. The problem of interpretation thus raised is one of great interest, with a view toward attempting to discover the sphere in which the spiritualization of prophecies takes place.

THE MIGHTY TYRE: PREDICTED TO BE DESTROYED

1. *The Prophecy:*

"Therefore thus saith the Lord God: Behold I am against thee, O Tyre, and they shall destroy the walls of Tyre, and break down her towers; I will also scrape her dust from her, and make her a bare rock. She shall be a place for the spreading of nets in the midst of the sea.... And they shall lay thy stones and thy timber and thy dust in the midst of the waters.... Thou shalt be built no more: for I Jehovah have spoken it, saith the Lord Jehovah" (Ezek. 26:3, 4, 5, 12, 14)[2].

2. *The Fulfillment:*

Tyre was one of the foremost neighboring cities, at the time of the theocratic government of God's covenant people. It was one of the great cities of the

---

[1] cf. A summary of them on page 26.
[2] All Biblical quotations in this book are from the American Revised Version, published by Thomas Nelson and Sons, and copyrighted 1929, by the International Council of Religious Education.

ancient world that stood opposed to the theocratic, holy nation. A very strategic position marked its location on the Mediterranean, so that its inhabitants became the foremost mariners, merchants, and explorers of antiquity. Though the Phoenicians aided Solomon in the building of the temple, they became a snare to Israel, on account of their Baal worship.

The particular form of the judgment on this city is given by Ezekiel. It is so specific that no one today would be safe in hazarding a prophecy as detailed concerning any city. The end of this city is foretold in a most circumstantial fashion. How was it fulfilled?

Tyre was besieged by Nebuchadnezzar, king of Babylon, and her walls and towers broken down. But the riches of the city did not fall into his hands, in any great measure. These the rulers of Tyre had transported to an island approximately a mile out into the sea. Nebuchadnezzar left the city in ruins, according to the prophecy. For it read, "They shall destroy the walls of Tyre and break down her towers."

But the rest of the prophecy was not yet fulfilled. Nor did it seem at all likely that anyone would undertake to cast her stones into the sea, her timber and dust into the water. Yet there was the prophecy.

For two hundred and forty years, the faith of God's people had to wait, after the seige by Nebuchadnezzar, for the further fulfillment of the prophecy. It seemed utterly incredible that this would take place.

But Alexander the Great, with his swift phalanxes, became the instrument of Jehovah, on the sandy shores of Old Tyre. A New Tyre on the nearby island refused his summons to open its gates to him. Its hardy mariners felt secure on their island citadel.

Meanwhile, Alexander the Great undertook the well nigh impossible and built a causeway to the island, using the stones of the Old Tyre, its timbers and its dust, in the mounds of the ruins left by Nebuchadnezzar. Accomplishing the prophecy, he cast these materials into the waters. Thus he built the roadway that enabled him to capture the city. God's Word was fulfilled.[1]

Today, after a period of over twenty-five hundred years, one may study the prophecy and visit Old Tyre to find it truly a place for the spreading of nets, for it is marked by nothing but sea-sand and an occasional piece of rock that looks like the ancient building stones so much in evidence at the excavated cities of Palestine.

Here then is a prophecy pointing forward to the far distant prophetic horizon of Ezekiel. But we see its fulfillment as before our eyes. It persuades us of the inspired, supernatural character of the Word of God, with a renewed joy of certainty.

And this instance brings home to us the problem whether not all prophecies must be fulfilled with the same literalness. It causes one to appreciate the evidence that can be adduced for spiritualization. We come to ask: *What must be spiritualized and what not?* But that question will have to wait, while we consider other instances.

---

[1] For the historical matters of this chapter, see G. T. B. Davis, Fulfilled Prophecies That Prove the Bible, 1931; J. Urquhart, The Wonders of Prophecy, 1925; A. Keith, De Stipte en Letterlijke Vervulling der Bijbelsche Profetiën, 1865.

Concerning Sources: That there are literal fulfillments is considered as granted by the Premillenarians. What remains to be proved is that there

SIDON ABIDING: THE PREDICTED BLOODSHED

1. *The Prophecy:*

"Behold, I am against thee, O Sidon .... For I will send pestilence into her, and blood into her streets; and the wounded shall fall in the midst of her, with the sword upon her on every side; and they shall know that I am Jehovah" (Ezek. 28:22, 23).

2. *The Fulfillment:*

The prophecy of Tyre could not be exchanged with that of Sidon, because of its very precise character. Nor could the fulfillments of these two prophecies be interchanged. For they form a most remarkable contrast.

The cities themselves sustained well-nigh the same relationship to the theocratic kingdom. In fact, Jezebel was the daughter of Ethbaal, king of the Sidonians. The city of Sidon became one of the greatest dangers for the northern Israelitish tribes, because of its idolatry.

On the prophetic horizon, Ezekiel sees much bloodshed in this city. Her wounded shall fall in the midst of her, by the sword on every side. But no doom of extinction is pronounced upon Sidon as upon her daughter and leader, Tyre.

The prophesied judgments, however, are abundantly confirmed by the checkered history of the

---

are spiritualizations and spiritual fulfillments and their scope in Scripture. Accordingly, this first chapter, dealing with literal fulfillments depends upon the recognized, historical, **secondary sources**, investigated and quoted at length by Urquhart. At the same time, the writer has made grateful use of Davis' presentation, to whom indebtedness is also acknowledged here. However, the writer's Biblical discussions, where not historical, have been developed directly from the **primary source**, — Scripture itself. (For Bibliographical Note see end of book.)

city. About 35 B. C., Sidon revolted against the Persians and was besieged by this people. "When all hope of saving their city was gone, 40,000 citizens chose to die rather than submit to Persian vengeance. They shut themselves up with their wives and children, set fire to their dwellings and perished amid the flames."

But this tragic event did not end the doom of suffering. More judgments were to follow. Thrice it fell into the hands of the crusaders and each time it was recaptured by the Moslems. One reads the prophecy of the sword upon her on every side, with a new interest.

Even in modern times, old Sidon marks the site of many conflicts between the Druses and the Turks and between the Turks and the French. In 1840, the city was bombarded by the combined fleets of England, France, and Turkey.

As the prophecy had not forecast the destruction of the city, so too history has not seen its destruction; but the foretold bloodshed corresponds with events in a truly remarkable fashion.

Should anyone be inclined to think that prophecy is of such a general type as to fit any fulfillment, let him but interchange the prophecies of Tyre and Sidon and then compare their histories. No human eye could have looked down the march of the centuries to foretell that old Tyre would be cast into the sea, in distinction from Sidon. Here again we may conclude with the words of our Lord, "Heaven and earth shall pass away, but my words shall not pass away." Thus Jehovah is glorified in the fulfillment of His Word.

And the problem of the literal fulfillment of prophecy again is shown to have its complexities.

Where must we expect literal fulfillment and where does the element of spiritualization enter in? The proper sphere of spiritualization is no doubt an interesting problem, to be considered in later chapters. However, let us first look at a few more instances of literal fulfillment.

JUDGMENTS FORECAST FOR SAMARIA

1. *The Prophecy:*

"Therefore I will make Samaria as an heap of the field, and as places for planting vineyards; and I will pour down the stones thereof into the valley, and I will uncover the foundations thereof" (Micah 1:6).

2. *The Fulfillment:*

Samaria, instead of Tirzah, was chosen by Omri, to be the capital of Israel, the northern kingdom. He began the building of the royal palace on the oval hill, that descends to the surrounding plain on all sides, before the land again slopes up to the nearby hills. These hills are so distant that no ancient means of war could shoot from them into the city.

Here Ahab "did evil in the sight of the Lord more than all that were before him," I Kings 16:30. Here Elijah announced the judgments of the Lord. Here both the wicked king and his infamous wife, Jezebel, came to their end, according to the word of the prophet.

Here the prophets of the Lord were persecuted and the evil worship of the golden calves aggravated by that of the Baals.

Today the foundations of the palaces of Omri, Ahab and Jeroboam II, as they stood adjoining one another, are uncovered, according to the prophecy. Vegetation grows on the hill-sides of old Samaria. The stones of the palaces have been thrown down and many of them have found their way to the valley below.

Many similar, remarkable prophecies with respect to other cities and Bible lands, have received *literal* fulfillments.

But that of Zion creates a *problem* all its own. Let us consider it next.

ZION TO BE PLOWED AS A FIELD

1. *The Prophecy:*

"Therefore shall Zion for your sake be plowed as a field" (Micah 3:12).

2. *The Fulfillment:*

Jerusalem, the most revered city of the world, was built on hills. Zion, the southeast hill, marked the old Jebusite fortress that afterward became the city of David and that was most densely populated, even in the days of our Lord. Moriah constituted the northeast height of the city and on it stood the temple and many royal buildings including the palace of Solomon and the traditional judgment hall of Pilate. The western hill also gradually became a part of the city as early as Solomon; and in our Lord's days it included the palaces of the Herods on the western wall. This wall was left, with the Herodian palaces, by the Romans, to show posterity what kind of a city it had been. We were privileged to see it in 1931. It is still there today, and evidently includes in part the wall that was rebuilt by Nehemiah.

For, before the exile, the Babylonians "broke down the walls of Jerusalem round about" (II Kings 25:10).

The rebuilt city, destroyed by the Romans, after having passed through many subsequent vicissitudes, saw much of its old wall restored in 1542 by Suleiman the Magnificent. But his architect did not restore the ancient wall around the old city of David, on the southeast hill of Zion. A large part of this hill, therefore, lies outside of the present city wall, though a portion of the ancient wall of David has been identified upon it.

The prophecy foretold that Zion would be plowed as a field. Even in the days of our Lord, it did not seem probable that this prophecy would ever be fulfilled, for Zion then marked one of the most populous parts of the city.

But there was shown to us the hill, outside of the walls — a collection of gardens, and plowed from year to year, as a field. Thomson, in *The Land and the Book*,[1] tells of the hill being decked with fields of ripe grain. No other part of Jerusalem is under cultivation, in that manner today. No other part of Jerusalem has a similar recorded history. But the prophecy of Micah has been literally fulfilled, improbable as it once seemed to be, with reference the once holy hill of Zion.

How about other prophecies, with respect to the Holy City? Must they all be taken literally, or is there a sphere for spiritualization, and if so, of what

---
1) Vol. I, page 540.

perspective does Zion then form a part? We find that there is a future of the kingdom, an eschatology of the theocracy, whose perspective leads on into the Church, by way of the spiritualization of all its elements as they fit into that perspective. Thus we see that Zion is spiritualized by the Scriptures, to fit into that perspective.

Meanwhile, the old hill of Zion has its own specific history. This history too becomes the theme of prophecy. Thus Zion should be plowed as a field, according to the Word of God unto Micah.

Of course, such literal fulfillments are not only a wonderful testimony to the truth of Holy Writ.

But the temptation lies at hand to conclude that all fulfillments must be equally literal, without testing such a conclusion by the Scriptures themselves.

In fact the position is sometimes taken that no other type of fulfillment can be considered than the literal. *But when we institute an investigation into the prophecies concerning the theocratic kingdom, in order to see inductively what kind of a perspective the Scriptures provide, we find every phase of this kingdom spiritualized in the Scriptures themselves.*

Space does not permit the inclusion of that evidence now, later chapters being concerned with that.

But the spiritualized kingdom of prophecy comes to be the glorious Church of our Lord and Savior, Jesus Christ. Are you, as a member of that church, even now, in some measure, glorifying your Saviour, according to the predictions? *Soli Deo Gloria.*[1]

---

[1] Chapter I was published, as an article, in "The Banner" of Feb. 24, 1933, and is here used by special permission of "The Banner."

CHAPTER II
THE CHALLENGE

Naturally, in the light of many literal fulfillments the question arises whether all prophecies must not be fulfilled in the same manner. This position is defended by many. The following defense is characteristic, in *The Calvinistic Character of Pre-Millennialism*.[1]

"Certainly, true Calvinism must wrestle loose from every insidious attempt of resorting to questionable hermeneutical methods to bolster up preconceived opinions.... In principle a scientific Calvinistic hermeneutics looks with distrust upon allegorizing and spiritualizing. Indeed this spiritualizing is a very slippery thing to handle: it is a measure of emergency that will help out of a corner. Even such a pronounced anti-chiliast as Kuyper intimates this when he warns against a 'soul-killing spiritualizing.' And he avoids it to the extent that he pictures the glory of the new heaven and earth in such material forms as will satisfy every Chiliast. Now it is true that rhetoric comes in for the claims of its figures of speech, but while these require careful discrimination we must keep the closest guard against the fundamental mistake of losing the essential even when it is expressed in figurative language. Maresius has remarked: 'Let it be far from us to make God

---

[1] A publication, typical of many, but selected here because of its intering references to Calvinistic writers. By the Rev. Gerrit H. Hospers. (First Edition.)

double-sensed ('diglotton'), or that we attach manifold meanings to His own Word, in which we should rather behold as in the very clearest mirror the simplicity of the Author Himself (Psa. 12:6; 19:8). Wherefore a single sense of Scripture, viz. the grammatical, is to be allowed, and then it may be expressed in any terms whether proper, or tropical and figurative.' Of course, the latter must be done under well conceived conditions and in accordance with the principles governing rhetorical figures.

"In accordance with these general principles of interpretation the distinctive doctrines of Calvinism have been found. But by the very same method, and to the very same extent, the distinctive doctrines of Chiliasm have been found too. The accredited Pre-Millenarian writers of the last decades are men of piety and unreserved fidelity to the Word. While their exegesis usually is not professedly determined by dogmatic considerations for fear these might militate against some Scripture, their findings can hardly be said to be repugnant thereto.

"How correct we are in these assertions appears from the exegetical labors bestowed upon Rom. IX and XI. These chapters contain much material from which the doctrines of the Sovereignty of God, of the Decrees, etc., are construed. To prove these doctrines Calvinists are very fond of taking the declarations of Scripture as naturally as possible. On reaching Rom. IX, 15-24, the Arminian has the greatest difficulty to avoid the cogency of its straightforward declaration. But it is remarkable how the same method applies to Chiliasm, and how it reaches its complex of doctrines in the same manner and in the

THE CHALLENGE

same proportion, with the same estimate of the rhetorical figures. And it is even more remarkable, as if the Holy Spirit would have it specially emphasized, that Rom. IX and XI brings its strong Calvinistic doctrine in direct connection with what we hold to be specific Chiliastic doctrine. These chapters declare as simply and as obviously for Chiliasm as for Calvinism, and it is just the Calvinist who blows hot and cold at the same time when he sublimates these plain declarations favoring Chiliasm into the dust clouds of a forced exegesis."

Can we prove that ours is not "a forced exegesis," an unscriptural interpretation? The evidence that the Scriptures support the spiritual view of the future of the theocratic kingdom is found in Chapters VIII and IX. Coming then to this kingdom, the introductory question of its nature, its character, is fundamental and vital.

CHAPTER III
"A KINGDOM OF PRIESTS AND A HOLY NATION"
Ex. 19:6; I Pet. 2:9

There are various prophecies, as we observed in Chapter I, that have been fulfilled *literally*. The adduced examples, with reference to ancient Tyre, Sidon, Samaria and Jerusalem illustrate this. These are not sporadic illustrations, but part of a larger body of prophecies that can be matched with *literal* fulfillments. This wider group of prophecies concern Edom (Is. 34:10; Jer. 49:16; Ezek. 35:3-9); Babylon (Is. 13:19-22; 14:23; 34:11; 47:1; Jer. 50:10-26; 51:25-36); Moab (Ezek. 25:11); Ammon (Jer. 49:2; Ezek. 25:3, 4); Ekron (Zeph. 2:4); Ashkelon (Zeph. 2:4; Zech. 9:5); Gaza (two miles west of present Gaza: Zeph. 2:4; Jer. 47:5); Bethel (Amos 3:14, 15); Egypt (Ezek. 29:15; 30:4-16); Philistia (Zeph. 2:1-6); Palestine (Lev. 26:30-33; Deut. 29:22; Is. 8:11, 12; Ezek. 36:33-35, as prophecies of woe; and perhaps as prophecies of weal, incipiently fulfilled: Ezek. 36:33-35; Jer. 49:6).

Will all prophecies be thus *literally* fulfilled? Frankly, this question is not easily ignored when one is privileged to view and to study many *literal* fulfillments, in Bible Lands. In Chapter II, moreover, we saw the claim pressed, from the premillennial side, that all prophecies are to be interpreted without spiritualization.

Yet it is clear that there are certain instances of

spiritualization. For practically all interpreters, even among our premillennial brethren, admit that the children of Abraham are spiritualized in Scripture, as in Gal. 3:29.

Now, therefore, the question comes up: *Which prophecies must be interpreted literally and which spiritually? This is an inquiry that repeatedly arises, both among those devoting their lives to the study of the Scriptures and among others of our leaders.*

How, for instance, must one interpret such a verse as the following: "Pray for the peace of Jerusalem: They shall prosper that love thee," Psalm 122:6? Is Jerusalem here no more than the ancient Holy City, whose landmarks played so large a role in Israelitish history?

To point to several instances of spiritualization, in the Scriptures, may still leave room for saying: But you cannot spiritualize the Holy Land, Israel, Zion or Jerusalem, and other items that are vital to the premillennial view. In fact, this is substantially the position advocated, by some. And our minds crave the truth.

Hence it may be of use to search and see whether there is Biblical evidence for the spiritualization of all the items that are considered vital to the premillennial view.

An attempt will be made in later chapters, especially in Chapter VIII to adduce this evidence. But the items of this evidence combine themselves into the theme of the theocracy, — that is the divine government of Jehovah over his ancient covenant people, over his "kingdom of priests," his "holy nation." Ex. 19:6.

This results in the spiritualization of the theocracy, the spiritualization of Jehovah's kingdom of priests, — his holy nation. It gives us the spiritual eschatology of the theocracy, the spiritual future of the kingdom.

And so, even if we should say that prophecies are fulfilled literally, as a rule, we find a series of exceptions to this rule, in the future state of Israel, in the eschatology of the theocracy, in the spiritualization of the kingdom of priests, — the holy nation. To study this matter will be our endeavor. In this chapter, we therefore consider the preliminary question, WHAT IS THE CHARACTER OF THE TYPICAL KINGDOM, what is the nature of the theocracy? This question is of fundamental importance in the history of redemption.

A. — FORMAL ESTABLISHMENT OF THE TYPICAL KINGDOM

As early as the Song of Moses, the kingship of Jehovah over his covenant people is implied, — "Jehovah shall reign forever and ever." Ex. 15:18.

But when the Lord historically chose Israel out of all the nations as His people, and when Israel as a nation accepted Jehovah as its ruler, Israel formally came under the theocratic government and received its theocratic, divine king. To this we are referred in Deut. 33:4, 5:

> "Moses commanded us a law,
> An inheritance for the assembly of Jacob.
> And He (Jehovah) became king in Jeshurun,
> When the heads of the people were gathered,
> All the tribes of Israel together."

"A Kingdom of Priests and A Holy Nation"   29

1. *Place and Time.* Now the questions arise, where was it that the heads of the people were thus gathered with the tribes of Israel and recognized the Lord as their ruler? And when was it, historically, that the Lord chose Israel out of all the nations, in order to rule this people in a theocratic manner?

These fundamental elements in the formal establishment of the theocracy are correctly found by Davis[1] in Ex. 19:4-9, when Israel is encamped at Sinai just before the giving of the decalogue.

2. *Manner: Proposal and Acceptance.* To Jehovah's proposal and acceptance, in Exodus 19, may be traced the relationship that occurs, in the prophets, of Jehovah as the husband of Israel. This proposal reads as follows: "Now therefore, if ye will obey my voice indeed, and keep my covenant, then ye shall be mine own possession from among all peoples, for all the earth is mine: and ye shall be unto me a kingdom of priests and a holy nation." Ex. 19:5, 6. The acceptance follows in the eighth verse, "All that Jehovah hath spoken we will do." Compare Jer. 2:2; Ezek. 16:60.

B. — THE RULE OF THE TYPICAL KINGDOM

1. *The ruling agents not only received their authority from God (Rom. 13), but the will of God was made known by special revelation.* If then we have here its formal institution, the question is

---

[1] Davis, Dictionary of the Bible, Article on Theocracy.

in order, in what precisely the essence of the theocracy consisted. The idea of the theocracy then, lies in this that the ruling agencies placed over Israel not only received their authority from above, Romans 13, as in the New England Theocracy, but that having been chosen by the Lord to their labors, they had to carry out His will as revealed through *special revelation,* paralleling various crises in the history of the nation. This revelation came first of all in the law given to this nation; and, further, through prophets and priests; and even directly to judges and kings.

2. *The Constitution or Fundamental Law of the Theocracy.* The constitution, or fundamental law, of the theocratic kingdom we find, with M. G. Kyle[1] in the Ten Commandments, for they are not only given directly in the chapter of Exodus following the formal establishment of the theocracy, but they are fundamental to all other laws promulgated to the nation.

3. *Chief Groups of Laws of the Typical Kingdom.* The most important provisions that were given by Jehovah, for the guidance of the theocratic government of Israel, can be subsumed under three groups of laws: the ten commandments or words, as the constitution; the legislative statute; and the judicial judgments.

Even modern law distinguishes statutes from judgments. There are the statutes of our legislatures and the judgments of our courts, familiar to every lawyer.

---

[1] Kyle, "The Problem of the Pentateuch."

Similarly the technical distinction between statutes and judgments occurs in Scripture.

Even the form and style of the Biblical judgments is quite different from that of the statutes. In fact the Biblical judgments have a literary style much like that of judgments in the Code of Hammurabi, where the form is variable but approximately as follows: If a man does so and so, then the punishment is so and so. The same form with variations occurs in Ex. 22.

C. — HUMAN AGENCIES PROVIDED FOR ISRAEL TO CARRY OUT JEHOVAH'S WILL

1. *Priests and Their Duties.* As king of Israel, Jehovah, further provided human agencies, to proclaim and carry out his will. To *the priests* he gave the duties of studying the law and of training the people in its observance. Lev. 10: 8-11, "And Jehovah spake unto Aaron saying, thou ... thy sons ... that ye may teach the children of Israel all the statutes which Jehovah hath spoken unto them by Moses"; Deut. 31: 9-11, "And Moses wrote this law, and delivered it unto the priests the sons of Levi ... saying ... thou shalt read this law before all Israel in their hearing."

Meanwhile, the ceremonial requirements of the law, which were thus enjoined upon Israel, gave the task unto the priests of presenting the typically redemptive sacrificial blood unto the Lord and of carrying out the other liturgical requirements of the ceremonial statutes.

2. *A Succession of Prophets to Offset the Fortune-tellers.* Not only do we find Moses, the prophet, announcing to Israel the special revelation by which Jehovah ruled the theocratic nation, but the Pentateuch provided for a succession of prophets compassing the same purpose, Deut. 18:14, 15. "For these nations, that thou shalt dispossess, hearken unto them that practice augury, and unto diviners; but as for thee, Jehovah, thy God hath not suffered thee so to do. Jehovah thy God will raise up unto thee a prophet from the midst of thee, of thy brethren, like unto me; unto him ye shall hearken." Over against the succession of heathen diviners, whom Israel must not consult, stands the prophet of Jehovah. Each successive generation of Israel must seek light from the prophet of the Lord of their day and age. Hence a succession of prophets will arise to instruct Israel, culminating in the Great Prophet like unto Moses.

3. *Kings and the Law of the King.* Finally, the Pentateuch contained the law of *the king*, of which the eventual kings were held to make a copy, Deut. 17:15-18. "Thou shalt surely set him king over thee, whom Jehovah thy God shall choose ... And it shall be, when he sitteth upon the throne of his kingdom, that he shall write him a copy of this law in a book ... " Thus it became very clear that even the kings were only human agencies provided for Israel by Jehovah, in order to carry out the divine will in the theocracy.

"A Kingdom of Priests and A Holy Nation"   33

D. CRITICAL VIEW OF THE THEOCRACY

1. *The theocracy is then regarded as not having existed until after the exile.* However the Biblical view not only forms the basis of the eschatology of the theocracy contained in the Old Testament, but it also definitely excludes the critical view which, if held would also seriously affect the treatment of the related eschatological materials.

   In his "History of Israel," Julius Wellhausen has a chapter on "The Theocracy as Idea and Institution."[1] Now he, and, with him, the critical school, denies the historical communication of the Pentateuch that the theocracy was instituted, through Moses, in the wilderness.

   Wellhausen teaches, on the contrary, that the theocracy first arose after the exile — such as it was. The following grounds for this view are advanced:

   a. He points to the many phases of the pre-exilic history of Israel that were out of harmony with the requirements of the theocracy.

   b. He argues from the post-exilic attempt to carry out the law more faithfully than it had been kept before the exile. Hence he considers the theocracy a late, post-exilic attempt to carry out the law, which then naturally he also considers as late.

2. *The Critical Position Controverted.* On the one hand, we are far from identifying the apostate phases, in the religion of Israel, with the religion required by the theocracy; while, on the other

---

[1] 1878; pages 411-425.

hand, we do not consider these apostacies any better evidence that the theocratic laws had not been enacted, than we consider the liquor history, in the United States, evidence that the 18th Amendment, and the Volstead statute, and the consequent judgments of the courts have never been part of our legislative fabric.

a. The existence of the laws is not disproven by pointing to wholesale trangression.

b. In fact, in the face of Israel's transgression, it was just the theocratic requirements that led to the rejection, for a time, of the nation in the exile.

c. Wellhausen's effort to bring the rise of the monotheistic theocracy into the time of the late history of Israel does not help him ahead one step fundamentally, in maintaining his naturalistic positions. One still has to make the fatal admission that the rise of monotheism remains a mystery, even when placed late.

d. In fact, this mystery does not yield to any solution but that of revelation.

It is the history of this revelation, as applied to the eschatology of the theocracy, that interests us now.

And then we consider not only the theocracy to have arisen early, but also the rise of eschatology of the theocracy to have occurred early, in Israelitish history. It is very important to emphasize this in our day, when these things come to be challenged even in conservative circles.

"A Kingdom of Priests and A Holy Nation" 35

3. *Eschatological Bearing of the Critical View of the Theocracy Rejected.*

   a. We, therefore, do not, with Wellhausen, relegate the great bulk of this prophetic eschatological material to a late date, in harmony with evolutionistic philosophy.

   b. Nor do we accept the post-millenarian view of the future, that the world is gradually getting so much better that it will finally reach the perfected state, as much evolutionistic philosophy implies.

   With Gunkel and Gressman,[1] we regard the Old Testament eschatology as having had an early rise. But if the eschatology of the theocracy arose early, it stands to reason that the theocracy itself, which is the basis of this eschatology, also had an early origin.

E. — THE END OF THE THEOCRACY

1. *Not Found in the Rise of the O. T. Kingship of Saul.* The *close* of the theocracy we do not find, with Spencer, in the rise of the Old Testament kingship at the time of Saul. For the theocracy contemplated a human kingship in Deut. 17:18. Though Saul was indeed, antitheocratic, David was a theocratic king, whose prevailing attitude became the standard of comparison for later kings, in the Scriptures.

2. *The N. T. Era Marks the End of the Theocratic Rule of Israel.* The end of the theocratic rule of

---

[1] cf. Hugo Gressmann, Mose und seine Zeit, Die Anfänge Israels, Die älteste Geschichtsschreibung und Prophetie Israels; Hermann Gunkel, Schöpfung und Chaos, Elias Jahve und Baal, Babylonische und biblische Urgeschichte; esp. Gressmann, Ursprung der isr.—jud. Eschatologie.

the Israelitish nation is marked by the transition of the New Testament era. Indeed, the sceptre would not depart from Juda, nor the ruler's staff from between his feet, until Shiloh would come, and unto him would the obedience of the peoples be, Gen. 49:10. He is the one to whom would be the judgment, Ezek. 21:27. The close of the theocratic kingdom is, therefore, synchronous with the rise of the N. T. eschatological kingdom.

The present kingdom of grace, together with its final consummation, in the kingdom of glory, is eschatological, from the Old Testament point of view, because it is on the distant horizon of future events, as revealed to the prophets.

The purpose of the theocracy, in this connection, was therefore to foreshadow both the present kingdom of grace, the church, and the future kingdom of glory, in the new heaven and earth, wherein righteousness shall dwell.

Hence Jehovah's gracious rule of his covenant people, in Old Testament days foreshadows the far more gracious rule of the Divine Messiah to come. We consider this typical feature, more specifically, in the next chapters.[1]

---

[1] Their brevity of form is due to the fact that the material has served as the basis of somewhat broader class lectures.

CHAPTER IV
PROPHETIC TYPES OF CHRIST AND OF HIS CHURCH

Much is made of typology in these days, and with good reason. For there are many types in the Scriptures, that point forward to the Christ. The future of the kingdom, in Old Testament prophecies, has much to do with these types.

It is a question of great importance how these types will be fulfilled. Do they have their fulfillment, on the one hand, in Christ's humiliation, his exaltation, his church and in the final judgment?

Or must we give emphasis, on the other hand, to a millennial reign of Christ, as the great fulfillment of these types?

Because this question is very important we shall now study what the Scripture presents to us, concerning the prophetic priestly and kingly types of Christ.

Or, to speak in terms of theocracy, we now come to a CONSIDERATION OF THE OFFICES OF THE THEOCRATIC KINGDOM THAT BECOME TYPICAL OF CHRIST, AND OF HIS CHURCH.

These theocratic offices, of prophet, priest and king, each received especial prominence in different ages. For example, the most prominent office of the theocracy, in Mosaic times, was that of prophet, since Moses himself stood in the foreground, as a prophet mighty in word and deed. But from the era of David to that of the exile, especially the king was in the lime light, as the outward manifestation of the theocracy. After the exile, however, the high-priest stood out most persistently, as the theocratic representative.

Most noteworthy, now, is the fact that when the prophetic office is the most conspicuous, in the theocracy, we find the typical representation of Christ expressed in terms of Moses, the prophet, like unto whom the Coming One would be, Deut. 18:15. On the other hand, when the royal office comes to be the most outstanding, the typology attaches itself to the king, for the great Messiah of Jehovah would be David's Son, 2 Sam, 7:13, in whom would be fulfilled the sure mercies of David, Isa. 55:3. Finally, when the post-exilic high-priest comes to the fore, Joshua, the High Priest, becomes typical of the Messiah, who would not only rule upon his throne, but would also be a priest upon his throne, Zech. 6:13.

Hence we observe that the outward manifestation of the theocracy largely determined the form that was predominant in the eschatological representation from age to age.[1] We now take up each of the theocratic offices in its rich typical, eschatological import.

THE PROPHETIC OFFICE AND ITS TYPICAL SIGNIFICANCE

After the formal institution of the theocracy, the first of the three theocratic offices that comes to the fore in history, is the prophetic office, in the person of Moses. Now the eschatology of the theocracy at-

---

1) Compare Riehm's Messianic Prophecy, Second Part.

taches itself to this historical circumstance, for Moses becomes a type of Christ.

A. *Moses and His Eschatological Significance.* This typical relation becomes articulate somewhat later, in the prophecy of a prophet like unto Moses, Deut. 18:15. The first eschatological message, therefore, concerning the Coming One, after the institution of the theocracy, describes him, in terms of the prophetic office, "I will raise them up a prophet from the midst of thee, of thy brethren, like unto thee; and I will put my words into his mouth, and he will speak unto them all that I shall command him."

a. A Farther Perspective. This prophecy involves the distant future of the Messiah, it concerns a prophet who will be a mediator of such a revelation as the Sinaitic, a mediator who, like Moses will be a prophet carrying out such broad official duties that this prophet will have royal and priestly tasks at the same time. For, Moses, as prophetic *lawgiver,* was entrusted with royal duties under Jehovah. And at the formal institution of the covenant, it was Moses, and not Aaron, that sprinkled the altar and the people with the blood of the Old Covenant, certainly a priestly duty.

b. A Nearer Perspective. In its nearer perspective, the present prophecy involves all the *prophetic* types of the Coming One, in the theocracy; for all these prophets were somewhat like Moses, especially in this respect that they, and not the idolatrous wizards or necromancers to which the connection, by contrast, refers, were to be consulted by Israel for the will of Jehovah.

B. *The Angel of Jehovah and His Prophetic, Eschatological Significance.* But the history of revelation with respect to the eschatology of the prophetic office does not stop short here. Besides Moses, and even above him, there was another Messenger of Jehovah, entrusted to the theocratic nation, to guide it through the wilderness.

For when Israel had forfeited Jehovah's favor, and when Moses, the prophet, had mediatorially offered himself as a vicarious sacrifice for the people, Jehovah did not accept this sacrifice, but sent his Messenger, saying, "Behold, mine angel shall go before thee." Ex. 32:34.

a. This Messenger, the Angel of Jehovah, appeared repeatedly, under Jehovah's theocratic government of Israel, as a prophetic intermediary, for revelational purposes, as unto Jehovah and Gideon, Joshua 5:14, 15; 6:2; Judges 2:1-5; 6:11-14. He inspires these great captains unto a holy warfare.

b. Though only by implication, the Angel of Jehovah is identified with the eschatological royal Lord of the temple, in Mal. 3:1, "And the Lord, whom we seek, will suddenly come to his temple, and the Messenger of the Covenant, whom ye desire, behold, he cometh, saith Jehovah of Hosts." The messenger of the Covenant, who is the messenger or angel of the Lord, is here identified with the Lord of the temple. He thus comes to be the Messiah, Himself, especially in the light of the New Testament.

c. The fact that he is distinguished in the O. T. from Jehovah, and yet appears in a group of passages that ascribe divine honor to him in various ways, is significant. Within the range of the Old Testament, this figure is thus surrounded by mysterious suggestions of deity somewhat analogous to those appearing in certain other prophecies of a Coming One. For the Son of David also is divine — David calls his son his Lord — if he is then his son, how is he his Lord? The Son of Man also involves superhuman characteristics, as he appears in Daniel's eschatological vision, 7:13.

And so, within the range of the Old Testament, this prophetic intermediary, the Messenger of Jehovah unto his theocratic nation, the Angel of the Lord, is more and more clearly identical with the coming Divine Messiah, the divine Son of David, the divine Son of Man, the divine Lord of His temple, the divine royal prophet of his people.

C. *The Royal Prophet, and His Eschatological Significance.* The men that were called to the prophetic office, in the theocracy, were not the only prophetic types of Christ.

For, though David was called to the royal office, he was not only a royal psalmist, but also, as in his Messianic psalms, a prophet, (Acts 2:30) of such a kind that he typified the greater Son of

David, not only in his royal character, but also in his prophetic activity.

a. David, the Royal Prophet, as Type. The typical and Messianic fortieth psalm is ascribed to David by its superscription. In this psalm royal and prophetic characteristics intermingle, in describing both David the type and Christ the antitype. There are references to prophetic work — to proclaiming salvation — references which fitted King David, in a measure, but which evidently have a higher, typical application to the promised Son of David —

"I have proclaimed glad tidings of righteousness in the great assembly;
Lo, I will not refrain my lips, O Jehovah, thou knowest.
I have not hid thy righteousness within my heart
I have declared thy faithfulness and thy salvation;
I have not concealed thy loving kindness and thy truth
From the great assembly." Psalm 40:7-10.

b. Christ, the Royal Prophet, as Antitype. What David here says, applies to himself, but far more fully to his antitype. For this psalm is recognized as Messianic in Hebrews 10:7, where the following well known lines are quoted:

"Then said I, Lo, I am come;
In the roll of the book it is written of me."

Though what is here said applied to David, it is written of the Christ only, in an adequate sense. Hence David describes Christ, the royal prophet in Ps. 40:7-10 quoted above, in such terms that he also attributes prophetic activity to him.

c. The Zeal of the Royal Prophet Brings Reproach. We, therefore, see in David, though in less degree than in Moses, a type of the coming Messiah, who would combine prophetic and royal functions. We have in him a type whose royal and prophetic zeal enabled him to say, — "The zeal of Thy house hath eaten me up. And reproaches of them that reproach thee are fallen upon me." Ps. 69:9. But when these words were applied to Christ, the antitype, John 2:17, at the cleansing of the temple, there was a still more marked prophetic and royal zeal in evidence than had been shown in the case of David. This prophetic zeal, however, had resulted in reproaches, even though the prophet, in David's case, was the royal anointed of the Lord, and though Christ was the King that came in the name of the Lord, Luke 19:33.

D. *The Eschatological Servant of Jehovah Performs Prophetic Service.* Reproaches for prophetic faithfulness also constitute the thread of the further eschatological deliverances concerning the Coming Prophet.

For not only is the eschatological figure of the Servant of Jehovah, in Isaiah given for "a light of the Gentiles" and "a covenant of the people," but Isaiah shows us this prophetic Servant also accepting such reproaches (Isa. 50:6):

"I gave my back to the smiters,
And my cheeks to them that plucked off the hair,
I hid not my face from shame and spitting."
(Isa. 42:6; 49:6; 50:6.)

a. Reproached for Prophetic Work, Isa. 50:4-6. These reproaches come to the Servant, in the wake of faithful prophetic work, for in preceding verses we read:

"The Lord Jehovah hath given me the tongue of them that are taught,
That I may know how to sustain with words him that is weary.
He wakeneth morning by morning, he wakeneth mine ear to hear
As they that are taught." Isa. 50:4.

b. He sustains with Words, Isa. 61 — This same prophetic role of sustaining with words him that is weary and heavy laden, as ascribed to the Messianic Servant, is now the thread taken up and developed with regard to the eschatological prophet.

For in Isa. 61, we read:
"The Spirit of the Lord Jehovah is upon me
Because Jehovah hath anointed me to preach good tidings unto the meek;
He hath sent me to bind up the brokenhearted
To proclaim liberty to the captives,
And the opening of the prison to them that are bound;

>   To proclaim the year of Jehovah's favor,
>   And the day of vengeance of our God; to comfort all that mourn;
>   To appoint unto them that mourn in Zion
>   To give to them a garland for ashes,
>   The oil of joy for mourning,
>   The garment of praise for the spirit of heaviness;
>   That they may be called trees of righteousness,
>   The planting of Jehovah, that he may be glorified." (Isa. 61:1-3.)

E. *The eschatology of the prophetic office involves* not only the individual prophet, but *also the collective body of the faithful.*

   a. This thought is expressed by Moses. With a wish that would once prove reality, the prophet Moses had expressed the desire:

   > "Would that all Jehovah's people were prophets,
   > That Jehovah would put his Spirit upon them." (Num. 11:29.)

   But a stiff-necked and rebellious nation was not yet prepared for the fulfillment of this longing.

   b. Taken up and amplified by Joel. This wish, however, makes room for a prophecy, certifying that very thing, under greatly altered circumstances. For Joel prophesies to a repentant Israel, not only the removal of the locusts and the gift of rain, but spiritual showers of blessings as well, bestowing prophetic gifts upon all flesh:

> "And it shall come to pass afterward,
> That I will pour out my Spirit upon all flesh;
> And your sons and daughters shall prophesy,
> Your old men shall dream dreams,
> Your young men shall see visions:
> And also upon the servants and upon the handmaids
> In those days will I pour out my Spirit."
> (Joel 2:28, 29.)

CHAPTER V
ROYAL TYPES OF CHRIST AND OF HIS CHURCH

Let us now proceed from the eschatology, the future importance, of the prophetic office to that of the royal office. We may here recall the principle that the future eschatological agent, whether king or prophet or priest, is predominantly represented in terms of the theocratic agent in the O. T. Kingdom that is the most prominent in a certain age. And so, when the kings arise, the kingly character of the Messiah is especially brought out — in many a Messianic prophecy. For the historical circumstances which mark the theocratic kings color their typical significance as this comes to light in prophecy.

A. *Earlier Kings and Their Typical Import.* The lives of the earlier kings, to begin with, provide circumstances utilized in prophecy. Various circumstances give occasions for prophecies of the most fundamental significance. These prophecies concern the eternal and universal sway of the great Messiah, the promised Son of David.

a. An Eternal House for David's Son. When David would build the Lord an house, we find the prophecy that the Lord would build him an eternal house,

"And thy house and thy kingdom shall be made sure forever before thee:

Thy throne shall be established forever."

(2 Sam. 7:16.)

b. Universal Sway of the Messiah as Typified in Solomon. In Psalm 72, which is ascribed to Solomon, ruler of many lands, appears the picture of the Ideal Son of David, and the antitype of Solomon, of whom it is said:

> "Yea, all kings shall fall down before him;
> All nations shall serve him."

B. *Later Kings and Their Prophetic Import.* The later royal prophecies are also attached to historic occasions, but increasingly transcend these occasions, as the theocratic kingship deteriorates.

a. God will build the fallen hut of David when his dynasty has declined, Amos 9:11. When Amos sees, on the prophetic horizon, the exile and the downfall of David's dynasty, he is given the prophecy of the rebuilding of the falling hut of David, and of the future rule over the remnant of Edom, that ancient inveterate, and typical enemy, which, however, David had conquered. (Amos 9:11.)

> "In that day will I raise up the tabernacle of David that is fallen,
> And I will close up the breaches thereof;
> And I will raise up its ruins,
> And I will build it, as in the days of old;
> That they may possess the remnant of Edom,
> And all the nations that are called by thy name,
> Saith Jehovah that doeth this."

b. The Vision of the Royal Glory of the Messiah, is greater than the departed glory of Uzziah had been, Isa. 6:1. In the year of the death of the renowned king Uzziah, who had, however, invaded the temple to burn incense, against the law of the Lord, Isaiah sees the Lord sitting upon a throne, high and lifted up and His train fills the temple. Isa. 6:1. The prophet here apparently received a vision of the royal glory of the Christ, for in John 12:41 we read that Isaiah saw his glory; and besides the glory of every king in the theocracy, including the evanescent glory of King Uzziah, was typical of the far greater and undying glory of the Son of David.

C. *The Royal Servant of Jehovah and His Messianic Import.* The royal eschatological figure not only transcends the deteriorating O. T. kings increasingly; but He is identified with the vicariously suffering Servant of Jehovah.[1]

After Isaiah *has* received the message of the coming servitude of the theocratic nation, in exile, when Israel will suffer many indignities, Jehovah gives the progressive revelation of the coming indignities which the greater Servant of Jehovah, Jesus Christ, will suffer, as Israel's representative and vicarious king. Isa. 52:13; 53:12.

a. Identification of the Royal Messiah with the Suffering Servant of Jehovah. Even apart from the New Testament evidence (Acts 8:32, 33; Gal. 1:4; I Tim. 2:5; Titus 2:14; Hebrews 9:28) it would seem that some Old Testament

---

[1] The argument here developed is identical with that of a paper read before the American Oriental Society, at the meeting in Urbana, at the University of Illinois, held March 16 and 17, 1928.

materials can be cited that have a cumulative force, directed toward equating the Servant of Jehovah with the royal Messiah, as the Book of Enoch equates the Servant with the Son of Man.[1]

b. Citation of Old Testament Materials.

Granted evidence: There is Isa. 53:12a, reading, "Therefore will I divide him a portion with the great, and he shall divide the spoil with the strong." Of this passage, Cheyne[2] says: "Thus the Servant of Jehovah becomes at last practically identical with the Messianic king."

But Cheyne adduces no further evidence than may be implied in this verse.

Further evidence: It is worth the effort, because of its importance to the eschatology of the theocracy, to inquire whether there is any other Old Testament material with the same general trust of identifying the Servant with the royal Messiah.

(1) We have then, first of all, Isa. 52:11-13, showing an Exaltation of the Servant, that astonishes kings,

"Behold, my servant shall deal wisely,
 He shall be exalted and lifted up, and shall be very high.
 Like as many were astonished at thee,
 (His visage was so marred, more than man,
 And his form more than the sons of men),
 So shall he sprinkle many nations;

---
1) cf. Deutero-Isaiah by Reuben Levy, pages 44-45.
2) See his Commentary, in loco.

Kings shall shut their mouths at him;
For that which had not been told them shall they see;
And that which they had not heard, shall they consider."

Since Isa. 53 is a sort of elaboration of these last three verses of the previous chapter, Cheyne's identification of the Servant with the royal Messiah, in 53:12, if correct, would logically lead to the same identification here.

(2) The Servant is Greater than Royal Cyrus of Isa. 52:1-11. Furthermore, we have the argument that the Servant is a royal figure, because the earlier part of chapter 52 shows the results of the royal work of King Cyrus as a background for the still more astonishing work of the Servant, verses 11-13. "Sing together, ye waste places of Jerusalem, for Jehovah hath comforted his people, He hath redeemed Jerusalem. Depart ye, depart ye, go out from thence." The mention of the departure to rebuild the waste places of Jerusalem suggests the mention of King Cyrus in chapters 44 and 45, where his measures are shown to result in rebuilding Jerusalem. Cf. the words: "That saith of Jerusalem, she shall be inhabited . . . and I will raise up the waste places thereof; that saith of Cyrus, he shall perform all my pleasure, Chapter 44. Cf. Ezra 1:7-10. Now from this political deliverance of King Cyrus, in 52:9-11, we may construe the background against which is pictured the still

more astonishing deliverance of the Servant, when kings shall stop their mouths at him. The picture of the Servant here is therefore all the more to be understood as implying royalty, because it is painted or fitted against this royal background. Hence the deliverance of the Servant bids fair to be a royal deliverance, and in this sense a Messianic deliverance.

(3) The Servant in Isa. 42:1-6 exercises royal power, to bring forth justice. We leave aside the question whether the Servant is here originally individual or collective, for in either case the main question is, whether he receives a royal commission among the nations. It is then said of the Servant that he shall bring forth justice to the Gentiles. He shall bring forth justice in truth and the isles shall wait for his law. Nothing could imply royal authority and a royal commission more clearly than that. And if the Servant appears here with royal implications, we may fairly conclude that he appears here with Messianic associations, since the Messiah was to be anointed as king.

In Isa. 43:10, the servant is collective, referring to Israel, 44:1. Hence Israel, as a servant of Jehovah, in Isaiah, also typifies, in a measure, the Messianic, royal and prophetic Servant, Jesus Christ.

(4) An Implied Identification of the Suffering Servant of Jehovah and the Messiah is Given in Isa. 55:3, 4. Cf. Isa. 43:10 and Isa. 42:4.

We have in Isaiah 55:3, 4 apparently as clear an identification of the Servant with the Messiah, as the equation between the Servant and the Son of Man in Enoch[1]. For in Isa. 55:3, 4 we have reference not only to the sure mercies of David, a Messianic reference, but also the promise that the Lord hast given this promised Son of David, whether individual or collective does not matter, for a witness to the peoples, a leader and commander to the peoples. Now these are predicates analogous to those of the Servant. With reference to the witness here, compare ch. 43:10, "Ye are my witnesses, saith Jehovah, and my Servant who I have chosen." Moreover, the idea here of a leader and commander to the people reappears in 42:4, with reference to the Servant; "The isles shall wait for his law, till he has set justice in the earth." With the substance of such predicates of the Servant ascribed to the Messianic figure implied by the sure mercies of David, we have here the one Davidic Messiah. Compare also Isa. 53:2, where the tender branch and the root out of a dry ground is identical with the shoot out of the stock of Jesse and the branch out of his roots, in Isa. 11:1.

(5) Passages outside of Isaiah Tending to Prove the same Principle to be True.

(a) Identification of the Suffering Servant and the Branch of the Davidic dynasty in Zech. 3:8, based on Isa. 4:2; 11:1; Jer. 23:5 and 33:15

---

[1] cf. Deutero-Isaiah by Reuben Levy, pages 44-45.

and the Servant Passages from Isa., chapters 42-53. There are certain passages outside of Isaiah, which tend to unite the idea of a suffering Servant and an anointed King. We mention first Zech. 3:8, in connection with Zech. 6:12, 13. In Zech. 3 we find the terms servant and Branch, as descriptive of the same individual, "For I bring forth my Servant, the Branch." (3:8). Both terms are apparently derived from earlier prophets, Branch from Isa. 4:2; 11:1; Jer. 23:5 and 33:15, and Servant, according to the opinion of various commentators, from the Servant passages in Isa. 42-53. Moreover there is some ground in the context for identifying the Servant of Zech. 3:8 with the Servant in Isa. 53. For the Servant of Zech. shall remove the iniquity of the land in one day; and of the Servant in Isa. 53, we read: "The Lord hath laid on Him the iniquity of us all." Again the work of the Branch cannot have its final fulfillment in Zerubbabel, for he did not remove the iniquity of the land in one day.

The author of the Targum admits that by Branch, Tsemach, the Messiah is meant. His words are: Yath avdi Meshicha deyithgelee, "My Servant, the Messiah, who shall be revealed."

If the Servant and the Branch are identified in Zech. 3, we have the royal dignity attributed still more clearly to "My Servant, the Branch" in ch. 6, for there the prophet says, "Behold the man whose name is the Branch ... and he shall sit and rule upon his throne."

ROYAL TYPES OF CHRIST AND OF HIS CHURCH 55

(b) Identification of the Messiah and the Sufferer in Dan. 9:26. A second passage, outside of Isaiah, which may unite the idea of suffering, as in the suffering Servant, with the idea of the Messiah may be found in Dan. 9:26, the anointed shall be cut off, for which the Syriac has nethqetel meshichah, the Messiah will be killed, and similarly the Vulgate: Occidetur Christus.

Summarizing, we wish to point out that there seems to be a cumulative argument for identifying the Servant with the Messiah, not only in Isa. 53:12, where the identification has been made by Cheyne, but also in other O. T. passages, as illustrated above. And hence we conclude that not only the N. T. but also the O. T. contains material that would equate the Servant with the Messiah. And if so, this should come first, methodologically, in the commentaries, before the mention of the N. T. material having the same import.

D. *Concluding Royal Messianic Prophecies.* The later royal prophecies emphasize increasingly the contrast between the coming royal Messiah and O. T. royalty.

a. This Antithesis is Especially Clear in the Prophecy of a Righteous Branch as Contrasted with the Unrighteous Rulers of the Dynasty of David, Jeremiah 23:5. We find that amid days when recent rulers of the royal house of David had proved unrighteous men, Jeremiah prophesies, by contrast, of the coming righteous Branch of the Davidic dynasty:

"Behold, the days come, saith Jehovah, that I will raise to David a righteous Branch, and He shall reign as king, and deal wisely and shall execute justice and righteousness in the land." 23:5.

b. Ezekiel Receives a Prophecy of One Whose Authority Shall Never be Overturned, 21:27, the Shiloh, "Whose (right) it is." After the kingdom of Israel and Juda have both been overturned, amid great changes and revolutions in secular history, we find Ezekiel receiving a prophecy that points to one whose authority shall never be overturned: "I will overturn, overturn, overturn . . . . until He come whose right it is, and I will give it to him." 21:27.

c. The Messiah's Abiding Kingdom, Typified by the Son of Man, is Contrasted with the Transient Worlds Kingdoms, Symbolized, in Dan. 7, by the Four Beasts. When Daniel lives amid the world monarchy of Babylonia, he receives the vision of four world monarchies arising out of the great mass of humanity, and typified by four beasts arising out of the sea; but in contrast with these world dominions, he sees one like unto a son of man, and unto him is given dominion, and glory, and a kingdom, that all peoples, nations, and languages should serve him: his dominion is an everlasting dominion, which shall not pass away, and his kingdom that which shall not be destroyed. 7:14.

CHAPTER VI
PRIESTLY AND SACRIFICIAL TYPES OF CHRIST AND OF HIS CHURCH

After the exile, the kings of the O. T. Kingdom disappear from history. This also marks a transition in the related prophecies. For then the eschatology of the kingship appears only with the future of the priesthood, and the latter flowers out more than ever.

We, therefore, now attempt to trace this future, this eschatology of the priesthood and of the sacrificial system, from the bud to the flower.

Now though the priest was typical of the Coming One, from the very beginning of the theocracy, he does not seem to figure in explicit Messianic prophecy, until after the rise of the kingship.

A. *Identification of the Priestly and the Kingly Figure.* We note that the priestly figure, is several times suggestively associated with and identified with, the figure of the eschatological king.

   a. The Figure of Melchizedek, Ps. 110, as Priest-King. The earliest illustration of this is the typical figure of Melchizedek, as interpreted by David in Ps. 110, where we have the eschattological priestking, after his order —

> "Jehovah saith unto my Lord,
> Sit thou at my right hand,
> Until I make thy enemies thy footstool . . .
> Jehovah hath sworn and will not repent,
> Thou art priest forever, after the order of Melchizedek."

b. The Priestly and Royal Servant of Jehovah, Isa. 53:10-13. This figure of the priest-king is carried forward in prophecy. Against the historic background of Israel's predicted and threatening servitude, we get the prophecy of the priestly Servant of Jehovah. This mysterious figure performs priestly work and is rewarded with royal honor. For as priest he brings a striking offering — his soul having been made an offering for sin, Isa. 53:10, he pours it out unto death, verse 12. But he shall be exalted, lifted up, and shall be very high. Kings shall shut their mouths at him. 52:11-13.

c. The Davidic Prince a Priestly Figure, Jer. 30:21. In Jeremiah 30:21, priestly prerogatives are attributed unto the prince of David's dynasty, — "And their prince shall of themselves, and their ruler shall proceed out of the midst of them; and I will cause him to draw near, and he shall approach unto me: for who is he that hath had boldness to approach unto me? saith Jehovah."

d. The Priest-King on the Throne, Zech. 6. But it is only in the second Jerusalem, with its prominent high priest, Joshua, alongside of Zerrubabel, that the priest-king becomes explicit in prophecy. Though Zechariah 6 completes this picture, it is suggested in Zech. 3, where we have not only the prophecy, that Joshua and his fellow-priests are typical men, but also the intimation that, in connection with the Branch of David's dynasty, the Lord will remove iniquity of the land in one day. (vs. 8, 9). The final and most explicit O. T. picture of the priest-king is, however, found in Zech. 6 —

"Behold the man whose name is the Branch,
And he shall sit and rule upon his throne,
And he shall be a priest upon his throne."

B. *The Priesthood and its Typical Importance,—Its Eschatological Bearing.* The priesthood as well as the priest-king, is the subject of various prophecies, reflecting more or less their historic background, and forming a history of revelation related to that background.

a. An international priesthood on the far horizon, Isa. 66:21. In the vivid prophecy, in which Isaiah, as it were, sees the exiles before his very eyes, he foretells an eschatological priesthood which shall fully correspond to the theocratic priestly nation of Ex. 19. For not only are the Jews that shall return after the exile to "build the old wastes" given the prophecy,

"Ye shall be named the priests of Jehovah;
Men shall call you the ministers of our God." Isa. 61:6.

But Isaiah's prophecy announces principles of such universalistic scope, that the returning exiles will be enabled to look upon their "brethren out of all nations," as also eventually to be represented in Jehovah's priesthood — "And of them also will I take for priests and Levites." Chapter 66:21.

b. The Levites not to lack a man as priest. Jer. 33:17, 18. Jeremiah, however, prophesies the continuance of the Levitic priesthood. But the historical circumstances form an illuminating background to this prophecy. For it was at the time when the Chaldeans were threatening King Zedekiah, the Davidic house, and the priesthood, that the word of the Lord came to Jeremiah, promising that neither the priesthood nor the Davidic dynasty should be totally extinguished. Such a prophecy was needed at that time.

"For thus saith Jehovah, David shall never want a man to sit upon the throne of the house of Israel; neither shall the priests, the Levites, want a man before me to offer burnt-offerings, and to burn meal-offerings and to do sacrifice continually." 33:17, 18. Whether this continually must be understood within the scope of the Millennium or within the scope of the theocratic nation is a question for later consideration.

c. The Zadokite priests on the nearer eschatological horizon. Ezekiel, who belonged to the priestly family, in the theocracy, received the task, as an exile among the exiles, of giving them a message that was largely concerned with the future of the sacrificial system. His place, in the history of the revelation, with respect to the future of the priesthood, must naturally also be approached from its historical background.[1]

Now the prophet Ezekiel, in chapter 44, verse 10 indicates that many of the Levites had, before the exile, gone "astray . . . after their idols." These Levites are relegated, in this prophecy, to the lower forms of service, at the sanctuary, "Yet they shall be ministers in my sanctuary, having oversight at the gates of the house, and ministering at the house; they shall slay the burnt offerings and the sacrifice for the people, and they shall stand before them to minister unto them. Because they ministered unto them before their idols. And they shall not come near unto me to execute the office of priest."

But the sons of Zadok had, before the exile, kept the charge of Jehovah sanctuary, and had not gone astray, like the other priests, in following idols.

They only, therefore, among the descendents of Aaron, shall have the honor of doing full service as priests. But the priests the Levites, the sons of Zadok, that kept the charge of my sanctuary, when the children of Israel went astray from me, they shall come before me to offer unto me the fat and the blood, saith the Lord Jehovah. 44:15.

These elements, therefore, have a bearing upon the immediate future of the theocracy, after the return from exile, though Ezekiel's

---

[1] Failure to do this has caused great difficulty, in the apprehension of this message. It is especially Harold M. Wiener that has pointed out the relation of Ezekiel's message to the more immediate future of the theocratic priesthood, in his Pentateuchal Studies, and in the International Standard Bible Encyclopedia, article on Priests and Levites.

vision also includes elements that apply to the more distant perspective of the eschatological, future kingdom.

d. The covenant of Levi of life and peace, Mal. 2:4, 5. With Malachi new circumstances again form the background of his prophecy as to the eschatology of the priesthood. For he sternly censures the priests of his day that "despise" the "name" of Jehovah, 1:6. But he sees a more hopeful future, that Jehovah's "covenant may be with Levi," 2:4, a covenant of life and peace, 2:5, according to which they shall teach the people wisely and spread abroad the knowledge of God, 2:3f, 6f; 3:3f; cf. 1:6; 2:1f, 8f.

C. *The Sacrifices and Their Future Significance.* The sacrifices of the theocracy, as found in Leviticus, need not be enumerated here. But they typify the Christ and their import in prophecy is rich and varied.

a. Sacrifices will be equal to prayer, praise, thanksgiving, righteousness and joy. Their eschatology is apparently influenced by the Psalms. For not only does Hosea, in an eschatological context say, "So will we render (as) bullocks, (the offerings of) our lips, 14:2. But the Psalms had previously equated prayer with sacrifices, in Ps. 141:2.

> "Let my prayer be set forth as incense before thee;
>
> And the lifting up of my hands as the evening sacrifice."

Similarly, the Psalms had identified sacrifices with praise, in Ps. 54:6; with thanksgiving, in Ps. 51:17; with righteousness, in Ps. 45:5; with joy, in Ps. 27:6.

b. Man's sacrifices insufficient. Micah 6:5-8. Micah also shows the fundamental insufficiency of the O. T. sacrifices, and therefore the need of something more final, "Wherewith shall I come before Jehovah? ... Shall I come before him with burnt offerings, with calves a year old?"

c. Sacrifices by non-Israelites, Isa. 19:21-23. Isaiah foretells the time when even the Egyptians shall worship together with the Assyrians, 19:23, and when "the Egyptians shall worship with sacrifice and oblation, and shall vow a vow unto Jehovah and shall perform it," 19:21. In that day Jehovah shall have extended the covenant blessings to these peoples, saying, "Blessed be Egypt my people, and Assyria the work of my hands, and Israel my inheritance," verse 25.

d. Sacrifices in a clean vessel, Isa. 66:20. With respect to the oblation of the children of Israel, Isaiah foretells that they shall bring it in a clean vessel, unto the house of Jehovah.

e. Sacrifices without the ark, Jer. 3:16. The ark with its mercy seat, upon which the sacrficial blood was sprinkled, also finds mention, in an eschatological passage of Jeremiah. "And it shall come to pass, when ye are multiplied and increased in the land, in those days, saith Jehovah, they shall say no more, The ark of the covenant of Jehovah; neither shall it come to mind; neither shall they remember it; neither shall they miss it; neither shall it be made anymore."

f. O. T. sacrifices by Levites, Jer. 33:18, on nearer horizon of O. T. times. But when Jerusalem is threatened and wasted by the Chaldeans, and the hope that the O. T. sacrifices would be resumed is well nigh gone, Jeremiah must give Judah the hopeful message, "neither shall the priest, the Levites, want a man before me to offer burnt-offerings, and to burn meal-offerings, and to do sacrifice continually," 33: 18. This *continually* is evidently limited within the sphere of the millennium or of the O. T. theocracy. Jeremiah also foretells (the sacrifices of) thanksgiving that shall be brought into the house of the Lord, 33:11.

g. O. T. sacrifices by Zadokite Levites, Ezek. 42: 13, on nearer horizon. Ezekiel's prophecy not only distinguishes between the future service of the priestly families that had served idols and of the Zadokites that had not. But it also predicts the sacrifices that shall form a part of this future service, 42:13, "the priests that are near unto Jehovah shall eat the most holy things . . . and the meal-offering, and the sin-offering, and the trespass-offering."

h. O. T. altar consecrated by proper sacrifices, Ezek. 43:19, on nearer horizon of O. T. times. In this vision we, furthermore, have a kind of dramatic transaction between Ezekiel and the future priests of the restored temple, bidding them to consecrate the altar by means of sin-offerings, 43:19f — "Thou shalt give to the priests, the Levites, that are of the seed of Zadok, who are near unto me, to minister unto me, saith the Lord Jehovah, a young bullock for a sin-offering ... Seven days shalt thou prepare every day a goat for a sin-offering ... Seven days shall they make atonement for the altar, to purify it; so shall they consecrate it."

i. O. T. sacrifices to be given by prince, Ezek. 45:17. In the vision of Ezekiel, the Prince also figures in connection with various sacrifices, including sin-offerings, at the different festivals, for he shall supply the beasts, to make atonement, 45:17 — "And it shall be the prince's part to give the burnt-offerings ... in all the appointed feasts of the house of Israel: he shall prepare the sin-offering ... to make atonement for the house of Israel." These sacrifices in the vision of Ezekiel, therefore, serve to purify, 43:26; to cleanse, 43:20, 22; to make atonement, 43:20, 26; 45:17. Cf. Ezra 3:2.

j. Sacrifices to be brought by Gentiles. Zech. 14: 16, 20, 21. Zechariah 14 has a prophecy involving sacrifices, but there is no mention of the Zadokites nor of sin-offerings, nor of making atonement. On the contrary, the concept of holiness is extended beyond its original ceremonial purposes, for "the pots in Jehovah's house shall be like the bowls before the altar. Yea, every pot in Jerusalem and in Juda shall be holy unto Jehovah of Hosts; and all they that sacrifice shall come and take of them, and boil therein." Though the prophecy of Ezekiel spoke of the house of Israel, for which atonement was to be made through sin-offerings, 45:17, here the picture of Zechariah is filled with Gentiles as well as Israelites, including "everyone that is left of all nations that came against Jerusalem."

D. *The Temple and Its Eschatological Bearing.* A varied representation, with respect to the future temple, or the future place of worship, and who shall be privileged to enter Jehovah's courts also greets us in the O. T.
   a. To it all nations shall flow, Isa. 2:2, 3. Isaiah's message, with its implications so universalistic as to meet the spiritual needs of the faithful remnant in exile, emphasizes a glorious future for the Gentiles, as well as for the Zion to be redeemed with justice, 1:27. For in the latter days, according to this prophecy, the temple shall find all nations flowing into it. "And it shall come to pass, in the latter days, that the mountain of Jehovah's house shall be established on the top of the mountains and shall be exalted above all hills; and all nations shall flow unto it." 2:2, 3.
   b. Israel's O. T. temple will exclude foreigners, Ezek. 44:9-11, on nearer O. T. horizon. There is variety, in Isaiah's point of view, from that of Ezekiel. We see that the latter prophet is concerned, as a priest in the exile, with the future purity of the temple service. For a message from Jehovah, bearing upon this ideal, he

PRIESTLY TYPES OF CHRIST AND OF HIS CHURCH 67

had therefore been providentially prepared. He is keenly aware of the past desecration of the old temple by the foreigners that had been brought in by the luxury-loving Israelites, to slaughter their sacrificial beasts for them, 44: 9-11. He is, therefore, psychologically prepared for the vision of Jehovah, in which these menial tasks are committed to the lower orders of the priests. But foreigners to perform them shall not again be introduced into the temple courts. "No foreigner, uncircumcised in heart and uncircumcised in flesh, shall enter into my sanctuary ... But the Levites that went astray, they shall slay the burnt-offerings and the sacrifice for the people ... "

c. Ezekiel's more remote perspective involves the living waters. Ezek. 47. Meanwhile Ezekiel's vision, including the temple and the river of the waters of life, evidently included also a more remote eschatological perspective, whether premillenarian or not.

d. Zechariah sees all nations represented, Zech. 14:16. Zechariah again includes, in the worship at Jerusalem the remnant of the Gentiles. More particularly does he represent this remnant as keeping the feast of tabernacles together with Israel. Now the feast of tabernacles was the first to be kept by the Captives under Joshua and Zerubbabel, after the exile, Ezra 3:4. When we bear in mind this historical background, we see a remarkable correspondence between this dramatic event, upon Israel's arrival, and the circumstance that the coming worship of the Gentiles in the day of Jehovah of Hosts is here predicted in terms of this same feast. "And it shall come to pass, that every one that is left of all the nations that came against Jerusalem shall go up from year to year, to worship the king, Jehovah of Hosts, and to keep the feast of tabernacles." 14:16.

e. No Canaanite in the Lord's house, Zech. 14:21, who remains Canaanite in worship. When we are further told, by Zechariah, that "in that day there shall be no more a Canaanite in the house of Jehovah of Hosts," in spite of the fact that he has just foretold that the remnant of all the nations that came against Jerusalem shall "worship" there annually, we again face a manner of speech calling for some interpretation.

f. Malachi's universal place of worship. Mal. 1:11. Finally, Malachi does not limit the temple to Jerusalem. For his prophecy predicts a universal place of worship, 1:11, "For from the rising of the sun even unto the going down of the same my name (shall be) great among the Gentiles; and in every place incense (shall be) offered unto my name, and a pure offering; for my name (shall be) great among the Gentiles, saith Jehovah of Hosts."

Here we have even a more universalistic representation compassed than in Isaiah. For there all nations would flow unto the mountain of Jehovah's house, while here all nations shall worship everywhere. But in Isaiah the universalistic message serves to enhance the future glory of the Zion that shall be redeemed after the exile. Here, in Malachi, however, the universalistic prophecy presents the ethical contrast of a future, universalistic, "pure" worship over against a contemporaneous, narrow worship that despised Jehovah's name, 1:6.

CHAPTER VII

WILL THESE O. T. TYPES BE FULFILLED IN PREMILLENNIAL FASHION?

A most interesting question lies before us. Must we entertain the Millennial hope, when we study these types? Let us see what this involves. It concerns certain principles of interpretation, but their test comes in their application.

What kind of a picture do they really give us of a premillennial reign of Christ?

Let us therefore now study these principles and their application.

A.—PRESENTATION OF THE PREMILLENNIAL PRINCIPLES OF INTERPRETATION

We are not only concerned with the history of the revelation concerning the future of the theocratic kingdom. For the interpretation, the exegesis, of this prophetic material is also part of our task.

And then one's interpretive principles are of great consequence. For the hermeneutical principle of the Premillenarians yields results of quite a different kind from the results that seem to be taken for granted in many a New Testament passage.

Let us therefore see what this principle is and to what results it leads when applied to the interpretation of the eschatology of the theocracy.

The great principle of interpretation advocated by the Premillenarians is that the literal sense of prophetic materials must be adopted. Applying this principle more definitely to the eschatology of the theocracy, the interpretive principles derived from it may fairly be stated as follows:[1]

1. *The literal sense of a prophecy, including its so-called imagery, derived from theocratic conditions, must be its divine intent, though this does not exclude ordinary figurative language.*

2. *But the ban must be put on the spiritualization of the elements of the Old Testament theocracy, in so far as this spiritualization is concerned with the prophesied future of the theocratic kingdom.*

3. *If then the literal intent of a theocratic prophecy cannot yet be fully matched by a literal fulfillment, this literal fulfillment of these unfulfilled prophecies must still be looked for.*

B. — IMPORT AND CRITICISM OF THE PREMILLENNIAL INTERPRETATIONS

1. *Import:* Now to what results do these principles of interpretation lead, in the consideration of the materials under discussion? Briefly put, the fulfillment of the prophecies dealing with the future glory of the theocracy overleaps Christ's first coming and the era of the church, largely ignores the new heaven and new earth and belongs in an expected earthly millennial age. Applying this more specifically, the following is involved:

The eschatology of the theocratic kingship, since not literally fulfilled, in most of its details, during Christ's earthly sojourn and the period

---

[1] Compare G. N. H. Peters, The Theocratic Kingdom, 1884, Vol. I, p. 47f.

of the church, still awaits fulfillment during the millennium.

a. This involves the physical return of the glorified theocratic king, to reign as the Messianic Son of David, not only over Palestine and Israel but also over all the neighboring kings of Israel's old enemies.

It therefore includes the return of Israel to Canaan, not merely as an historic occurrence, but as an occurrence required by the introduction once more of the theocratic regime.

It similarly requires the return to their old habitat of all Israel's old enemies, under their kings, who, though still sinful, will be ruled by the Son of David.

b. It leaves sinners amid the sanctified of Israel and sinners in the nation round about.

c. It includes, necessarily, the literal fulfillment of those prophecies which show war as the means of reducing and keeping under the ancient hostile neighboring nations of Israel, the Israelites shall fly upon the shoulders of the Philistines, to introduce and to maintain this peaceful millennial age, Isa. 11:14.

d. It involves, meanwhile, the tameness of ferocious animals and the glorified state of plant life in the Holy Land. But the rest of the world is not yet rid of its thorns and thistles.

e. The sacrificial system as shown in the prophecy of Ezekiel (chapter 40f), in Zech. 14 and elsewhere, shall be introduced.

This includes the reintroduction of sacrifices, including sin- and trespass-offering, though Premillenarians attempt to explain that these sacrifices will not serve for atonement, since Christ's atoning work is regarded as complete.

f. It includes the building of the temple shown to Ezekiel, and the river of the waters of life, taken literally.

g. It involves that the faithful from all nations shall come to Jerusalem, for the feasts, according to the ancient mode of travel, on dromedaries and swift horses.

2. *Criticism of These Interpretations.* Now, this position is evidently in conflict with itself, in several respects.

a. For though the millennial offerings are regarded as having no atoning implications, the offerings in Ezekiel's vision serve to make atonement, 43:20, 26; 45:17, to cleanse 43:20, 22; and to purify 43:26. On the millennial position, there should be no sin- and trespass-offerings, in the millennium, whereas Ezekiel's vision includes both, 43:13, 19f. The sin- and trespass-offerings are placed after Christ's atonement, which, if it were correct, would evidently nullify the finality of the latter.

b. With respect to the *place*, the location of the ceremonial service, the literal interpretation again runs into contradictions. Isa. 2 and Zech. 14 bring all the nations or their remnant to Jerusalem for worship, while Malachi authorizes their presenting to God in every place incense and a pure offering, 1:11.

c. Again, on this interpretation, Ezekiel limits the millennial priesthood to the sons of Zadok, while Jeremiah speaks of the priests, the Levites, without any such limitation, and Isa. 66, according to many commentators, allows for priests being taken from the Gentiles, in a very universalistic fashion.

d. Once more, millennial peace is undisturbed by the claw of a wild animal, but the theocratic people shall fly, in battle, upon the shoulders of the Philistines, Isa. 11:14.

e. A glorified Messiah, shall be able, as a prophet, like unto Moses to see all the sin of the unsanctified around him, without condemning it in such unsparing terms that no Calvary or Judgment Day occurs, nor any judgments like those inaugurated by Moses in the wilderness.

f. A glorified Holy Land shall be able to lie amid a world not yet glorified, yet the thorns and thistles of the rest of the world shall not turn the new Garden of Eden into a garden with thistles.

h. Though passages like Gen. 12:3; Isa. 42:5-16; Zeph. 3:15, are regarded in the New Testament as fulfilled, the Premillennial position is that these must yet be fulfilled in the Millennium. (Luke 2:32; Acts 13:47; Acts 26:18.)

C. — CONCLUSIONS AS TO THE CONTRADICTORY INTERPRETATIONS THUS ARISING

We are, therefore, clearly brought to the general conclusion that, on this view, it remains a profound mystery how, and amid what sort of circumstances, Christ would carry out, during the Millennium, the tasks of His threefold office at Jerusalem, — as its great prophet, its vicarious high priest and its glorified king.

1. *Concerning Our Lord's Prophetic Work:*
   The conclusion has become perfectly clear, as to Christ's prophetic work, that it involves various contradictions, in the performances of its duties, on the purely literal interpretation.

    a. For why should not our own Lord Jesus Christ, as the great prophet, like unto Moses, if he should come down from heaven, in the Millennium, unto sinners, in and around Palestine, bring about repeatedly during the Millennium, judgments like unto those of Moses in the wilderness? Or would sin no longer deserve punishment? Or is there not enough sin in the naturally depraved heart and life to call for punishment?

    b. And although the Messiah made like unto us except for sin, in his state of humiliation, might willingly suffer in his spirit, because of the presence of sin, for the sake of being a friend of publicans and sinners, what right have we to expect the glorified Messiah to come down to earth to suffer thus again in the Millennium?

2. *Concerning Jesus' Priestly Activities:*

The conclusion is also apparently inescapable that Christ's priestly offices involves various contradictions, in the performance of its duties, if all the prophecies concerned are to be understood literally.

a. For did not Christ present himself as a sin offering[1] and a trespass offering[2] and thus make a final and complete atonement for our sins? But how then can Christ continue to make atonement[3] in the Millennium? Hence how can Christ require his representatives, the priests,[4] to continue to make atonement, in the Millennium, by means of sin offerings[5] and trespass offerings?[6]

b. It is therefore clear that Ezekiel's great temple vision[7] includes elements on the nearer Old Testament post-exilic horizon, as well as elements on a more distant horizon.

The restoration, at Jerusalem, of sin offerings and trespass offerings, making an atonement, typically,[8] in the post-exilic days of Joshua,[9] the high priest, and Zerubbabel, the prince,[10] certainly belong to the nearer Old Testament horizon.

It is, however, equally clear that this same great temple vision of Ezekiel includes ele-

---
1) 2 Cor. 5:21.
2) Isaiah 53:10.
3) Millennial view of Ezek. 43:20, 26; 45:17 expects their fulfillment in the Millennium.
4) Ezek. 42:13; 43:19.
5) Millennial view of Ezek. 43:19 f.
6) Millennial view of Ezek. 43:13.
7) Ezek. 40-48.
8) Zech. 3:8.
9) Zech. 3:8; Ezra 3:2.
10) Zech. 4:6; Ezra 3:2; 1:8; Ezek. 45:17.

ments referring to the farther New Testament horizon, and the farthest horizon of the new heaven and new earth. Such elements are involved in the temple[1] and the river of the waters of life.[2]

For the temple here appears without the veil, suggesting that the veil has had its day, and has been rent in twain. Now the New Testament temple is the church.[3]

And the river of the waters of life suggest the living waters that Christ announces.[4] If one drinks from the well of Jacob[5] one will thirst again in this life and in the life to come.[6] But if one drinks of the living water[7] one will never more thirst. We should, therefore, come unto Christ for the living waters.[8] We may even begin to enjoy them, here and now, in this present world. But they shall be enjoyed, clear as crystal,[9] unsullied and perfectly pure, in the new heaven and new earth,[10] in which righteousness shall dwell, as the living waters flow from the throne of God and of the Lamb. When we get there, it will be early enough to find out whether these living waters from the throne of God have also a literal meaning. That they have a spiritual meaning is certain. This is without

---
1) Ezek. 40:5; 44:1; 47:1.
2) Ezek. 47:9.
3) Hebr. 9:2; 2 Cor. 6:16; 1 Peter 2:5.
4) John 4:10.
5) John 4:6.
6) Luke 16:24; John 4:13.
7) John 4:14.
8) John 7:37.
9) Rev. 22:1.
10) Rev. 21:1.

a doubt their chief and most important message to us now.

c. Again it is perfectly clear that the Zadokite[1] priesthood of Ezekiel fits the nearer horizon, after the Babylonian exile.

For then the high priest, Joshua, the son of Jozadak,[2] of the descendants of Zadok,[3] served at the altar.

To expect the children of Zadok to serve at the altar once more, in the Millennium, is without scriptural evidence, and one of the apparent absurdities to which a purely literal interpretation of prophecy leads. For some of elements of Ezekiel's great temple vision were not fulfilled after the exile, such as pertain to the size and proportions of Ezekiel's visionary temple. Hence the whole temple and all its Zadokite priests and offerings must needs, on this view, await its complete literal fulfilment in the Millennium. However, we hold that God's prophetic word may be considered true, though it never takes place literally, in a Millennium,[4] that sin and trespass offerings are presented at the altar, by a Zadokite priesthood. These elements fit the nearer Old Testament post-exilic horizon.

d. Meanwhile the universal priesthood of Isaiah,[5] extending even to the Gentiles, certainly presupposes Isaiah's more distant

---
1) Ezek. 43:19.
2) Ezra 3:2; Neh. 12:1, 8; 1 Chron. 6:15.
3) 1 Chron. 6:4-15.
4) cf. point 3, page 71.
5) Isa. 66:21.

prophetic horizons of the New Testament and of the new heaven and new earth.

But understanding every prophecy literally, the picture of the future priesthood creates a hopeless confusion and contradiction, for the Millennial age.

8. *Concerning Christ's Royal Office:*
And, finally, as to Christ's kingly office, the conclusion is also clear and apparently inescapable, that it involves various contradictions, in the performance of its tasks, if all the prophecies concerned are to be interpreted literally.

a. Would not Christ's royal dignity lead to the judgment day on the throne of his glory, with the goats on the left and the sheep on the right,[1] long before the Millennium would come to an end, if the glorified kingly Christ were bodily present with sinners of all sorts?

b. If his Israel would need to fly upon the shoulders of the Philistines,[2] to introduce the Millennial age, would these Philistines not need the same kind of rough treatment repeatedly, in the (peaceful) thousand years, if we may compare the Philistines of Iraelitish history?

Certainly, the native Arabic speaking population of Palestine today, representing apparently the mixed descendants of the old Philistines and Canaanites, especially, are not very friendly to Israel. Witness the strifes between these Arabic natives and the Jews, in connection with the Wailing Wall at Jerusalem. The

---
1) Matt. 25:33.
2) Isa. 11:14.

Jews will apparently have to fly upon the shoulders of those Arabic speaking Philistines many a time, to keep their rebellious spirits subdued.

Or will the natural man, and especially the natural Arab or Philistine, change his nature, or the leopard change his spots?

D. — TRANSITION TO THE STUDY OF THE EVIDENCE FOR DETERMINING THE BIBLICAL SCOPE OF SPIRITUALIZATION

For all these difficulties there is the solution offered by the Scriptures themselves, in the scope that the Scriptures give to the principle of spiritualization, while they also recognize the scope of literal fulfillments.

The evidence for the scope of spiritual fulfillments and of literal fulfillments we are to consider in later chapters, especially in the eighth.

Nor are these difficulties and contradictions that are affirmed in the Old Testament, on a literal interpretation of prophecy, reaffirmed in the New Testament, or explained by the New Testament in such a way as to require the literal fulfillments of all these prophecies. Quite the contrary is the case, as is evidenced in Chapter IX.

Nor does, notably, Revelation 20, where the thousand years are mentioned, reaffirm these contradictions and difficulties. This fact is of the greatest importance for the proper interpretation of the prophecies.

In the light of all this evidence, there is, as we shall see, a different way in which the Scriptures foretell that Christ shall be the great prophetic and priestly king of Zion. Because of the fact that Christ's kingship is illumined by his prophetic work, and based upon his priestly task, the main and final question, as to the future of the kingdom, can be summarized as follows: How would Christ become king of Zion, according to the prophecies, — in an exclusively literal premillennial fashion, or, within a certain scope, in a spiritual manner?

The evidence for the latter position is taken up in the next chapter, and involves an inductive study of the scope of spiritualization. The question is taken up, — for how much spiritualization is there evidence in the Scriptures?

Now it is clearly quite essential that this investigation shall be directly based upon the Biblical evidence for such spiritualization; and also that it shall be systematic, aiming to cover the entire scope of what is actually spiritualized by the Scriptures, by the Holy Spirit, their author.

For though there is always a practical usefulness in adducing but a few illustrations of spiritualization, nothing less than a fairly complete treatment of *all* the elements spiritualized by the Scriptures can serve as evidence on the question: What is the Biblical scope of spiritualization?

And precisely an inductive determination of this Biblical scope of spiritualization is necessary for the interpretation of the prophecies dealing with the future of the Old Testament kingdom, as it is typical of the New Testament kingdom.

On the other hand, though we or the Millenarians may adduce various instances of literal fulfillment, this does not prove that there are no instances of spiritualization, also in the Scriptures.

And so, from this approach, the question again arises, What then is the Biblical scope of literal fulfillments and of spiritual fulfillments?

How, in general, can one tell whether a prophecy is to be interpreted literally, or whether the spiritual fulfillment is sufficient to meet the requirements of the prophecy? These questions are now to be considered in the next chapter.

They all, naturally, converge toward the most prominent question concerning the future of the typical kingdom: How would Christ become king of Jerusalem, according to the prophecies?

CHAPTER VIII

HOW THEN WOULD CHRIST BECOME KING OF JERUSALEM?

That the Messiah would become king of Jerusalem, of the Promised Land, of Israel, yea, of his entire kingdom is clearly foretold, in Scripture,[1] and confessed by Premillenarians with enthusiasm.

That he would become king, by way of his humiliation and vicarious suffering is equally clear, in Holy Writ, and admitted as well by our Premillennial brethren. We thank God for this.

The great question, accordingly, under consideration here, is *how* Christ would become king, if not Premillennially? In other words, if the Premillenarian view leads to the difficulties and contradictions summarized in the previous chapter, does Holy Writ show the way out of these difficulties?

If so, how then would Christ become king of Jerusalem?

Hence the great question is, how would the prophecies be fulfilled, dealing with this kingship.

That clearly depends upon the manner in which the complete hope of the O. T. saints would be realized. We, therefore, consider that broader question here. And then we find that this hope would be fulfilled in a spiritual fashion.

---

[1] cf. 2 Sam. 7:16; involving the prophecy of a kingdom without end, forever, Isa. 9:7; on the throne of David, Acts 2:30, fulfilled by Christ's sitting at the right hand of the Father, Acts 2:33.

For every one of the elements of the Theocracy is spiritualized in the Scriptures, though the Premillenarians have denied that such is the case with the most crucial of these elements, such as Israel, the Kingdom, the Holy Land, Zion and others.

What is meant by spiritualization, or the spiritual interpretation, in this connection? The spiritual interpretation, here concerned, is that which is contrasted with the view of the Premillenarians, who hold to the so-called literal interpretation, — happily not consistently, as a rule.

Though the presentation of the *evidence* for the spiritualization of Zion, Israel, the Promised Land, and all the other items connected with the kingdom is of fundamental importance, yet it will make for clearness to analyze first the *meaning* of the spiritual interpretation, here intended.

I. MEANING OF THE SPIRITUAL INTERPRETATION, OR THE BIBLICAL SPIRITUALIZATION, APPLYING TO JERUSALEM AND TO OTHER ELEMENTS CONNECTED WITH THE TYPICAL KINGDOM.

This spiritual interpretation or spiritualization may have direct, Biblical evidence, or not. If it has, it may naturally be regarded as a Biblical spiritualization. If it lacks explicit, Biblical evidence, but rests on sound logic, it may be considered as an inferential spiritualization. Thus some have inferred that, because the children of Abraham have been spiritualized in Scripture, therefore one may, by inference, also spiritualize Israel. But this inferential evidence is not as convincing as the direct teaching of Scripture concerning Israel, especially not among people of Biblicistic[1] leanings. Moreover, the argument here is exegetical, as basic to the more inferential, dogmatic type of argument. Hence our first concern will be to seek for the Biblical spiritualization, rather than the inferential.

In the Scriptures, the Holy Spirit, as the primary author, frequently interprets his own terms, so that the so-called literal interpretation fails to do justice to the broad meaning that the Spirit literally gives to the abiding elements associated with the typical, Old Testament, theocratic kingdom, for these elements reappear in connection with the New Testament antitypical kingdom, in spiritualized fashion.

Now we are here concerned, especially with the future of the typical, theocratic kingdom, in prophecy and fulfillment.

By the spiritual interpretation, in Scripture, is, therefore, meant, here, the interpretation that the Holy Spirit gives to the various items connected with this kingdom. Such interpretation requires us to search the Scriptures, in true Berean fashion, not only for the literal meaning of these items or terms, but also for the special import, or broader meaning, or richer implication that the Spirit gives them.

In the spiritual interpretation of Scripture, *we*, therefore, do not simply allegorize the meaning of Scripture. For such allegorization would be

---
[1] cf. Dr. William H. Rutgers, "Premillennialism in America," p. 150-155, and Dr. Ralph Bronkema, "The Essence of Puritanism," p. 80-124.

the work of man. What the spiritual interpretations in Holy Writ require, on the other hand, is the interpretive work of the Holy Spirit himself. Allegorization may proceed without evidence and without bounds. But the spiritual interpretations in the Word of God need the evidence given by the Spirit and are bound by that.

Again, the spiritual interpretations in Scripture are not the same as mere metaphorical interpretations, for the latter also might be only the work of man. Moreover, though the spiritual interpretations in Scripture do include some figurative language, they are not limited to that.

For the Biblical spiritualization of any item, connected with the typical, Old Testament kingdom, includes any special import, or broadened meaning, or figurative usage, or richer implication that the Holy Spirit gives to this item, with a view toward realizing the fulfillment of the typical, Old Testament kingdom, in the antitypical, New Testament kingdom, as identified with the church, both here, and in eternity, hereafter.

Biblical evidence, that an item is given a broader or special sense, fitting in with this entire trend of spiritualizations, thus remains the main requirement, as evidence for each individual, Biblical spiritualization.

An item, then, is spiritually interpreted, in this sense, because its literal meaning has been enriched, in some way, by the Holy Spirit, and because the specific evidence for that enrichment can be adduced, from Scripture.

How Would Christ Become King of Zion? 87

This Biblical enrichment of the literal meaning of a kingdom-item is considered to be a spiritual interpretation of the item, because it is the work of the Holy Spirit, primarily; and, secondarily also, because it leads toward or to the higher spiritual levels of the antitypical New Testament kingdom, or even to the highest spiritual levels of the final kingdom of glory, when time shall be no more.

All this is more clearly expressed by the term spiritual interpretation than by spiritualization. But spiritualization has come to be used in the sense of spiritual interpretation. And its brevity is an advantage, in the following brief and summary treatment of the evidence. More Biblical quotations might be cited than those presented here. Meanwhile, the attempt has been made to exclude, as evidence, any Biblical passages not perfectly clear.

II. PRESENTATION OF THE EVIDENCE THAT THE SCRIPTURES INTERPRET SPIRITUALLY JERUSALEM, THE PROMISED LAND, ISRAEL, EVEN ALL THE ABIDING FEATURES CONNECTED WITH THE TYPICAL O. T. KINGDOM THAT REAPPEAR IN CHRIST'S KINGDOM.

Let us now turn to the evidence for this complete spiritualization, showing that Christ would be the Spiritual king of his spiritual Zion, the Church, amid the spiritual counterparts of the entire Old Testament kingdom, the theocracy.

For it is naturally a matter of the greatest

consequence that we find not only some of these elements spiritualized, as is readily granted by the Premillenarians, and has been frequently demonstrated, but that we find: THE ENTIRE THEOCRACY SPIRITUALIZED BY THE SCRIPTURES.

And so there is abundant Biblical evidence that the principles of interpretation, the hermeneutic principles themselves, of the Premillenarians, are open to objection, as applied to those elements that the Premillenarians refuse to spiritualize.

A. — THERE IS A LATENCY OF SPIRITUALIZATION IN THE O. T. AND AN EVIDENT SPIRITUALIZATION IN THE N. T. OF THE PERMANENT ELEMENTS CONNECTED WITH THE TYPICAL KINGDOM THAT RECUR IN "THE KINGDOM OF THE SON." (Col. 1:13)

A fundamental Biblical difficulty with the Premillenarian positions is, evidently, that the insistence upon a literal interpretation of the Old Testament prophecies, dealing with the future of the kingdom, leads to ignoring this latency of spiritualization in the Old Testament as well as this evident spiritualization in the New, for the entire theocratic kingdom. For all the vital elements are thus spiritualized.

1. *Zion and Jerusalem.*

   a. Latent spiritualization in the O. T. Isa. 49:14; Isa. 51:3; 52:1, 2. Let us begin with Zion, as an example. Zion is, in the Old Testament not only the city Jerusalem, but also the people of

God, whether they had ever lived in Jerusalem or not, — even when viewed in their exilic desolation, far away from Mt. Zion, and as dispersed abroad in the provinces of Babylonia—. Isa. 49:14, "But Zion saith, Jehovah hath forsaken me and the Lord hath forgotten me." Zion is here the Lord's people, which he has comforted, according to the preceding verse, and which formerly had gathered to worship at Zion, but is now addressed as in exile.

Isa. 51:3, "For Jehovah comforted Zion, He hath comforted all her waste places." By Zion here, we must understand the former worshippers at Jerusalem, the descendants of Abraham and Sarah (verse 2), who have drunk at the hand of Jehovah the cup of his wrath (verse 17), but Jehovah will now put it into the hand of them that afflict Zion (verse 23). Thus again the idea of Zion is broadened to include the children of Abraham, exiled to regions far from the city of Jerusalem. Zion here suggests the covenant people, though far from the waste places of their ancient home.[1]

Jerusalem as well as Zion is thus used, Isa. 52:1, 2, "Awake, awake, put on thy strength, O Zion, put on thy beautiful garments, O Jerusalem, the Holy city . . . the captive daughter of Zion." Here the captive people of Jerusalem is summoned to shake itself from the dust of the captivity, to cast away the chains (verse 2), to depart from the land

---

1) For Zion in Isa. 28:16 see Psalm 87:5 and I Peter 2:6.

of exile, for Jehovah will go before them and the God of Israel will be their rearward (verse 12). Glorious is the era of strength and beauty (verse 1) that will come to Zion, to Jerusalem, here addressed as in the captivity.[1] Thus, far from the holy land, the covenant people is here addressed as Zion and Jerusalem, a broadened use of these terms, — preparing for their more general New Testament usage, as applying to the church.

How rich also is the meaning of the psalmist:

"Pray for the peace of Jerusalem:
They shall prosper that love thee."
Psalm 122:6.

b. Evident spiritualization in the N. T. Gal. 4: 26; Heb. 12:22; Rev. 3:12; Rev. 21:9f. The New Testament spiritualizes Zion and Jerusalem outright and so makes it representative of Gentile as well as Jewish Christians, — Gal. 4:26, "But the Jerusalem which is above is free, which is our mother," Hebrews 12:22, "But ye are come unto Mt. Zion and unto the city of the living God, the heavenly Jerusalem." Rev. 3:12, "And I will write upon him the name of my God and the name of the city of my God, the New Jerusalem, which cometh down from heaven."

There is certainly an identification of Jerusalem and even of Israel with the Church, in

---
1) In the Apocrapha, Zion is also used for the captive people of Judah. — 2 Esdras 2:40; 3:2, 31; 10:20, 39, 44.

Rev. 21:9f., — "Come hither and I will show thee the bride, the wife of the Lamb." Now N. T. usage describes the Church[1] as the bride of Christ. But here John says: "And He showed me the Holy city, Jerusalem, coming down from God having twelve gates ... and names written thereon, which are the names of the twelve tribes of the children of Israel." This identifies Jerusalem, including its gates named for Israel, with the church, evidently spiritualizing the theocratic capital, Jerusalem. Thus the Messiah's foretold Kingship over Zion becomes his Kingship over the Church. In this sense, Abraham also "looked for a city, which hath foundations, whose builder and maker is God," Heb. 11:10.[2]

2. *The Holy Land as the Inheritance of the Covenant People.*

   a. Latent spiritualization in the O. T.; Num. 18:20; Deut. 18:2; Ps. 73:26; 16:5; 142:5; 119:57; Jer. 10:16; 51:19. Again there is a latent spiritualization of the holy land in the Old Testament. The tribes of Israel receive a portion of Canaan as their inheritance. But Jehovah is the portion, the inheritance of the priests: Num. 18:20, "And Jehovah said unto Aaron, Thou shalt have no inheritance in their land, neither shalt thou have any portion among them: I am thy portion and thine inheritance among the children of Israel." Similarly Jehovah is the inheritance of all the Levites, Deut. 18:2, "And they shall have no

---
1) cf. Rom. 7:4; 2 Cor. 11:2; Eph. 5:23-33.
2) cf. Page 144.

inheritance among their brethren. Jehovah is their inheritance, as he hath spoken unto them."

Asaph, one of these Levites, expresses further his personal spiritual appropriation of Jehovah as his inheritance, Ps. 73:26, "My flesh and my heart faileth, But God is the strength of my heart and my portion forever."

But so does also David, who was not a Levite, Ps. 16:5, "Jehovah is the portion of mine inheritance." Ps. 142:5, "I cried unto thee, O Jehovah; I said Thou art my refuge; My portion in the land of the living."

The writer of Ps. 119 expresses a similar faith in verse 57: "Jehovah is my portion."

Meanwhile Jeremiah applies this principle to all of Israel, 10:16 and 51:19: "The portion of Jacob . . . Jehovah of Hosts is his name."

Hence we see that in the Old Testament the primary inheritance, the real portion of Israel was not Canaan, but Jehovah himself, and only in a secondary way whatever Jehovah might give unto his people.

b. Evident spiritualization in the N. T.: Mat. 5:5; Rom. 4:13; Col. 3:24; Gal. 3:29; Heb. 9:15; 11:10; 1 Peter 1:3-5. While there is thus a latent spiritualization of the holy land, as the portion of Israel's inheritance in the Old Testament, we see an evident spiritualization of the inheritance of Jehovah's covenant people carried forward in the New Testament.

The limitation to Canaan disappears, — "Blessed are the meek for they shall inherit the earth," Matt. 5:5. "For not through the law was the promise to Abraham or to his seed, that he should be heir of *the World,* but through the righteousness of faith," Rom. 4:13.

Gentiles will share in the inheritance, Col. 3:24, ... "knowing that from the Lord ye shall receive the recompense of the inheritance;" Gal. 3:29, "And if ye are Christ's, then are ye Abraham's seed, heirs according to promise."

The inheritance is "eternal," Heb. 9:15 ... "a city which hath foundations whose builder and maker is God." Heb. 11:10. Thus Abraham's inheritance is spiritualized, 11:8. It virtually includes Jehovah, and the new heaven, Heb. 11:10, and new earth, Rom. 4:13, Matt. 5:5.

This inheritance is earned by Christ and it centers in Him, I Peter 1:3. It is an inheritance, I Peter 1:4, incorruptible, 1:4, 18, undefiled, 1:4, 19, and that fadeth not away, 1:4, 24, but is as eternal as Christ and His word, 1:18, 19, 24. As Jehovah was the great portion of his covenant people in the Old Testament, so their inheritance receives still greater vividness in the New Testament, in Christ Jesus, our portion forever. And shall not the Father with him give us all things, both the new heaven, Heb. 11:10, and the new earth, Matt. 5:5, as our inheritance?

Thus the Messiah's prophesied rule over the land of Israel's inheritance becomes his rule over the new heaven and new earth.[2]

---
1) cf. Page 147.

3. *The Kingdom.*
   a. Latency of spiritualization. Ex. 19:5, 6; Isa. 19:25; Ps. 74:12; Isa. 43:15; Ps. 2:8. There is also a latent spiritualization of the kingdom in the Old Testament. For in Ex. 19:5, 6, we read, "If ye keep my covenant, . . . ye shall be unto me a kingdom. . . . " Now the predicates of the covenant are applied in Isa. 19 to the Gentiles of the future, — "Egypt my people, and Assyria, the work of my hands, and Israel, mine inheritance," Egypt, the people of "Jehovah of hosts," (Isa. 19:25) is therefore also expected to live up to the covenant obligations, implied for Jehovah's people. And Assyria comes under similar obligations and privileges. These nations are representative of the great Gentile world, to which the covenant privileges will therefore be extended. But then Ex. 19 must also apply in this wider sphere, — "If ye keep my covenant . . . ye shall be unto me a kingdom. . . . " There is therefore here clearly in evidence a latency of spiritualization, with respect to the Kingdom, in the Old Testament.

   This latency of spiritualization appears still more strongly, if we read on in Ex. 19, — "ye shall be unto me a kingdom of priests . . ." Now a kingdom of priests strikes a spiritual note, it shows the fundamentally spiritual character of that kingdom, even in those theocratic days before the outward rule of David's house had appeared. This kingdom of priests existed apart from any earthly dynasty. This is perfectly evident from its exclusively spiritual requirements, — "Now, therefore, if ye will obey my voice indeed, and keep my covenant, then . . . ye shall be unto me a kingdom of priests . . . " Though the kingdom and the covenant are here interrelated in a fundamentally spiritual way, that applies eschatologically to the Gentiles as well.

This spiritual character of the kingdom is progressively reinforced also elsewhere, for in Ps. 74:12, attributed to David, God as king is looked upon far more in a spiritual way than in a political, for there we read, "God is my king of old, working salvation in the midst of the earth."

And from Isa. 43:15 we must conclude that Jehovah's rule is especially intended to be that of the inner spirit that dedicates itself to the Holy one of Israel; "I am Jehovah, your Holy One, the Creator of Israel, your King."

b. Evident spiritualization. Matt. 21:43; Matt. 8:11; Eph. 2:12; and Col. 1:13. On the other hand, the kingdom can go on without Israel. It can be taken away from Israel and given to a nation bringing forth the fruits thereof. For the eschatological kingdom already fundamentally spiritual in the Old Testament is thus spiritually interpreted in the New. For Matt. not only reports Christ as teaching that the vineyard shall be taken away and let out to other husbandmen who shall render him the fruits in their season; but, in the following context, we get the practical bearing of this statement, — "The kingdom of God shall be taken away from you and shall be given to a nation bringing forth the fruits thereof." (Mat. 21:43). In the previous section, the vineyard would be merely let out to other husbandmen. But here the kingdom shall actually be taken away and given. Certainly the Pharisees caught the point, when they sought to lay hands on Jesus. For the kingdom would be taken away from them.

Not only is the kingdom of God here thus spiritualized and generalized, instead of being indissolubly associated with Israel after the flesh. But the same applies to the kingdom of heaven, — Mat. 8:11, "Many shall come from the east and west, and shall sit down with Abraham, Isaac, and Jacob, in the kingdom of heaven, but the sons of the kingdom shall be cast forth into outer darkness."

Paul carries out the same idea, by describing the Ephesians as formerly "alienated from the *commonwealth* of Israel," (the commonwealth here covering the kingdom), but now "fellow *citizens* with saints," how could this mean anything else than fellow citizens of the kingdom? Eph. 2:12 and 19.

Hence it will hardly do to say: The kingdom is within you, — that is, its king is in your midst. But the inward character of the kingdom is here emphasized, as elsewhere, where we read that the kingdom is not a matter of Jewish ceremonies, not meat and drink, but righteousness, peace and joy. Rom. 14:17.

Again, when Christ says that his kingdom is not of this world, kosmos, else would his followers fight, it will hardly do to interpret that Christ's kingdom is not of this age, 'aioon, but of the millennial age. Certainly the millennium would be no time to fight, though there will still be unconverted sinners, according to the current view.

On the contrary, that kingdom is not of this world, for it cometh not with observation.[1]

Thus the kingdom over which the Messiah would rule is a spiritual kingdom.

4. *The Seed of Abraham, as the Covenant People, Heirs of the Kingdom.*

   a. Latent spiritualization in the O. T. There is also a latency of spiritualization with respect to another theocratic term, the seed of Abraham, in the Old Testament. For the Pentatouch does not limit Abraham's seed to his descendents, but even his servants are included in the covenant. Moreover, proselyes could be added.

   But the spiritualization of Abraham's seed also works in the other direction, in the Old Testament, limiting the concept to the faithful. Hence Ishmael and Esau drop out. Hence Lo-ammi, Not-my-people, and Lo-ruhamah, Not-pitied, in the prophecy of Hosea.

   b. Evident Spiritualization in the N. T. Gal. 3:29 and Rom. 4:12; cf. also Rom. 9:27. Meanwhile,

---

[1] cf. John 18:36.

this spiritualization of Abraham's seed goes forward apace, in the New Testament. Paul writes to the Galations, 3:29, "And if ye are Christ's then are ye Abraham's seed," and to the Romans, 4:12, "that he (Abraham) might be the father of all them that believe."

The New Testament spiritualizes Abraham's seed also in an exclusive fashion, for Paul quotes, "neither, because they are Abraham's seed, are they all children, but in Isaac shall thy seed be called," Rom. 9:7, evidently sharing this kind of spiritualization with the Old Testament.

Hence, the seed of Abraham, whom the Messiah would rule, become the believers.

5. *The Covenant-People as the Bride of the Lord.* Both the Old Testament and the New represent God's covenant people as his bride. If the true Israel and the invisible church are identified, in the New Testament, as one covenant people, this naturally results in one bride, a position which is infinitely better than the logical premillenarian position of two brides[1] of Christ, in the future, Israel and the Church.

a. The figure of the bride incipiently applied to Jehovah's spiritual covenant people in the O. T. theocracy. The national covenant at Sinai was first presented in the form of a proposal, "Now, therefore, if ye will ... keep my covenant, then ye shall be mine own possession from among all peoples," Ex. 19:5. Isaiah

---

[1] cf. Scofield Bible, 1917, page 922, concerning Hosea 2; quoted by the Rev. D. Zwier, in De Wachter, Vol. 66, No. 39.

makes the figure of the bride explicit, "Where is the bill of thy mother's divorcement?" 50:1. It appears repeatedly with reference to the spiritual Israel in Isaiah, Hosea, Jeremiah and Ezekiel.

b. The figure applied to Christ's spiritual followers, whether of the true Israel or of the invisible Church.[1] John the Baptist uses the figure, John 3:29, 30, "He that hath the bride is the bridegroom; but the friend of the bridegroom, that standeth and heareth him, rejoiceth greatly because of the bridegroom's voice: this my joy therefore is made full. He must increase, but I must decrease." Jesus also uses the figure in Mat. 9:15, "The days shall come when the bridegroom shall be taken away from them, then shall they fast." In Rev. 21:9-12 the bride of Christ, evidently the church, is identified with the true Israel: "Come hither and I will show thee the bride, the wife of the Lamb . . . And he showed me the holy city, Jerusalem . . . and at the gates twelve angels; and names written thereon, which are the names of the twelve tribes of the children of Israel." Certainly here the Lamb does not appear with one bride, representing the Church and another, representing Israel, but there is reference here to only one bride, evidently identifying the covenant people of Israel, and that of the Church, into one invisible church, one spiritual Israel, one Bride.

---

[1] cf. Rom. 7:4; 2 Cor. 11:2; Eph. 5:23-33.

Thus the one eschatological covenant bride of the Messiah is his church, the spiritual Israel.

6. *Israel, the Covenant People, Recipients of the Kingdom.* With Israel, the situation is not essentially different than with various other items spiritually interpreted by the Scriptures, though the Premillenarians would have one think so.

For to the Gentile proselytes of the covenant, incorporated into Israel in the Old Testament, correspond the Gentile believers, united with the spiritual Israel of the New Testament. This final, augmented Israel is contemplated also in various O. T. prophecies.

a. *Latent Spiritualization of Israel in the O. T.*

This is found in both the law and the prophets. In the law, we read, explicitly, of the privilege of the proselytes of righteousness to be incorporated into Israel. For even the privilege of partaking of the passover is accorded to them. "And when a stranger shall sojourn with thee, and will keep the passover to Jehovah, let all his males be circumcised, and then let him come near and keep it; and he shall be as one that is born in the land. One law shall be to him that is home-born and unto the stranger that sojourneth among you. Thus did all the children of Israel." Ex. 12:48-50.

Among the prophets, Isaiah stands supreme, in giving a spiritual interpretation to Israel, by prophesying the incorporation of Gentiles, into the covenant people.

In Isa. 44, we have a prophecy that many of the Gentiles will surname themselves by the name of Israel, after it has been restored and laden with blessings, and that especially they will accept Israel's God: "One shall say, I am Jehovah's; and another shall call himself by the name of Jacob; and another shall subscribe with his hand unto Jehovah, *and surname (himself) by the name of Israel.*" 44:5.

Thus Jehovah will unite in one body those that were formerly at the greatest variance, so that they all shall count it the greatest honor to belong to Jehovah, as members of his spiritual Israel. (Cf. Calvin's Commentary.)

This prophecy involves an initial application to the Old Testament proselyte of the covenant; but it also has a broader basis of application, in the Gentiles of the New Testament day that publicly profess their allegiance to Jehovah, and their incorporation into his covenant people, Israel.

More than a dozen excellent commentaries could be mentioned that all interpret Israel as thus inclusive of Jew and Gentile, in this verse, — the Gentile adherents thus being merged with the covenant people of Israel, though each nationality remains distinct.

This abiding distinction of the nationalities is also clearly implied by Isaiah. For, though Israel is frequently called Jehovah's people, the work of his hands, his inheritance, yet these three epithets severally are applied not only to Israel, but also to Assyria and to Egypt: "Blessed be Egypt, my people, and Assyria, the work of my hands, and Israel, mine inheritance." 19:25.

Thus the highest description of Jehovah's covenant people is applied to Egypt, — "my people," — showing that the Gentiles will share the covenant blessings, not less than Israel. Yet the several nationalities are here kept distinct, even when Gentiles share, in the covenant blessing, on a level of equality with Israel. Egypt, Assyria and Israel are not nationally merged. And the same principle, that nationalities are not obliterated, by membership in the covenant, applies, of course, also in the New Testament dispensation.

It is also possible, according to the prophets, for some Israelites, to lose their place in the covenant, and to fall to the spiritual level of Gentiles outside of the covenant: Amos 9:7, 8, — "Are ye not as the children of the Ethiopians unto me, O children of Israel? saith Jehovah. Have not I brought up Israel out of the land of Egypt, the Philistines from Caphtor, and the Syrians from Kir?"

Similar are the words of Isaiah: "Except Jehovah of hosts had left unto us a very small remnant we should have been as Sodom, we should have been like unto Gomorrah. Hear the word of Jehovah, ye rulers of Sodom; give ear unto the law of our God, ye rulers of Gomorrah." Isa. 1:9, 10.

The same principle of Israel's abiding nationality applies in a different way in the texts where it is foretold that Israel will possess the nations, as in Isa. 54. Here "the Holy One of Israel" speaks to his Israel[1], which is practically identical with his faithful Zion.[2] Its tent must be made wide, — especially from the time of its post exilic restoration and on into the N. T. day. The true Israel, when restored, shall increase in numbers, yea they shall even possess the nations. In the light of the N. T.[3] that possession includes the present authority of Christ over his believers, Jewish and Gentile alike, a spiritual rule, in the church.

We thus learn from Isa. 54:1-5 that Israel shall possess the nations. However we need not go to the N. T. to see how spiritual this possession will be and how the responsive Gentiles shall be incorporated into the Spiritual Israel though they may remain nationally distinct. Isaiah could not have put this more plainly than he does in Chapter 56:3, "Neither let the foreigner, that hath joined himself to Jehovah speak saying: 'Jehovah will surely separate me from his people.'" This therefore teaches just the opposite from spiritual separation. One covenant people of Jew and Gentile results, not two, kept spiritually separate.

---
1) cf. Isa. 54:5.
2) cf. Isa. 52:1, 2.
3) cf. Acts 15:17, interpreting Amos 9:12. See page 168.

It naturally results in a spiritual seed of Israel that includes both the Jew and Gentile foreigner.

This is also clearly implied in another passage from Isaiah, — 45:22-25. "Look unto me and be ye saved, all ye ends of the earth, for I am God and there is none else."

The exhortation, "look unto me," evidently includes Gentiles in the light of the verses 6, 14 and 22, referring to Egypt, Ethiopia and the Sabeans.

But Isaiah goes on to say: "Only in Jehovah is righteousness and strength, even to him shall men come. In Jehovah shall all the seed of Israel be justified and shall glory."

Since the previous scene described in these verses embraces the whole human family, it is obvious that we are to understand by the seed of Israel here the spiritual posterity of the patriarch, both the believing Jews and the responsive Gentiles that heed the exhortation.

The reference to the seed of Israel here is thus clearly to the Israel of God out of all the human race, that is to the body of the believers in Israel expanded by the addition of the believing heathen, which body is now righteous, reconciled and renewed by Jehovah, and glories in him, because by grace it is what it is.

In other words, the Gentiles from the ends of the earth are here exhorted to look unto Jehovah and to be saved for there is none else, and to be incorporated into the true seed of Israel, for there is no other covenant people.

Thus the Lord turns himself to the Gentiles as well as to the Hebrews. To him they must turn, because he invites all the ends of the earth to turn unto him. For only in Jehovah is righteousness, and in Jehovah all the seed of Israel shall be justified, including the Gentiles that have given heed to the exhortation.

From all the above passages two conclusions may be drawn. On the one hand, the spiritual Israel, as the covenant people does not efface national lines, no more than the church does. On the other hand this spiritual Israel precludes such spiritual division in its midst as to result in more than one covenant people, for Gentiles are incorporated into Israel and among the seed of Israel. Ex. 12:48-50. Isa. 44:5, 45:25, 56:3.

b. *Evident Spiritualization of Israel in the N. T.*

Christ hath broken down "the middle wall of partition," Eph. 2:14, between Israel and the Gentiles, who were formerly, "afar off" and "alienated from the commonwealth of Israel." 2:12.

Hence there is a spiritual merging into the one "body of Christ" (1 Cor. 12:27), namely "the Church" (verse 28), both from those that are Israelites by nature and from those that are not. "For in one spirit they were all baptized into one body, whether Jews or Greeks." 1 Cor. 12:13; Col. 3:11.

Now on the one hand, "they are not all Israel that are of Israel." Rom. 9:6.

For there are some "that say they are Jews and they are not, but are a synagogue of Satan." Rev. 2:9.

But on the other hand though in the tame olive tree representing, "Israel" (Rom. 11:17), there are some Israelitish branches that are broken off, there are also others that remain, as well as Gentile branches that are grafted into the same olive tree.

Again this shows that into the true Israel represented by the olive tree, are incorporated the Gentile believers, to produce a spiritual unity, though national distinctions remain.

Now the question arises, does the New Testament apply this only to the present era, or also the prophesied eternal glory?

We find the twelve tribes of Israel identified in Rev. 21 with the bride of Christ, which is clearly the church.

For the angel says to John on Patmos, "Come hither and I will show thee the bride, the wife of the Lamb." And John sees "the holy city Jerusalem, having twelve gates, and names written thereon, which are the names of the twelve tribes of Israel." Rev. 21:9-12.

Thus the church, the bride, the wife of the Lamb is identified with Israel, and it is clear that the Gentile believers have been identified with the true Israel. Hence, again, the spiritual Israel and the church have been merged into one spiritual body, one covenant people.

But there is more evidence, in the N. T. Scriptures, that the true Israel and the church are thus intended to be identified.

For the Epistle to the Hebrews, which contrasts the two great dispensations of the Old Testament and the New, quotes a prophecy of Jer. 31, mentioning Israel and applies it to the church.

"For this is the covenant that I
 will make *with the house of Israel*
After those days, saith the Lord;
I will put my laws into their mind
And on their heart also will I write them
And I will be unto them a God,
And they shall be to me a people," Hebr. 8:10.

Now the fulfillment of this prophecy is sketched in the following elaboration and applied to *"the church" in 12:23*, — again identifying the true Israel with the church. Thus Israel is incorporated into the church.

On the other hand, the church members are also incorporated into Israel, in Ephesians 2:12 and 19. For though they were formerly *"alienated from the commonwealth of Israel,* (Ephes. 2:12), they are now *"fellow-citizens with the saints"* (2:19), *evidently fellow-citizens in the commonwealth of Israel,* the spiritual kingdom of Jesus Christ, according to Paul (Col. 1:13).[1]

Thus the Israel that was to be ruled by the Messiah is the spiritual Israel, the church of Jesus Christ, whose we are and whom we serve.

---
1) cf. Page 150.

7. *Israel's Enemies, for example the Edomites:*
   a. Latent spiritualization in O. T. Obadiah 1:15f; Isa. 34:5. Not only do Israel, the seed of Abraham, the kingdom and the temple receive this Old Testament spiritualization, supported by the clearer light of the New. But Israel's enemies receive similar treatment. Let us take one example. Edomites are representative of the enemies of God, in general, as in Obadiah, (verses 1, 15f) "Thus saith the Lord, Jehovah, concerning Edom ... For the day of Jehovah is near upon all the nations: As thou hast done, it shall be done unto thee; thy dealing shall return upon thine own head. For as ye have drunk upon my holy mountain, so shall the nations drink continually;" Isaiah similarly generalizes, beginning with the Edomites, 34:5, "For my sword hath drunk its fill in heaven, behold it shall come down upon Edom, and upon the people of my curse to judgment."

   Here we have Edom, not merely as a nation, but as exemplifying, in a prominent way, those that drink of the cup of the divine wrath, because of their great opposition to the kingdom of God. For Jehovah curses those that curse his people.

   Hence, when the Lord is said to come from Edom, he comes in the attitude of the wrath that Edom has deserved. This means that when Jehovah is said to come from Edom he comes with the wrath that he visits upon the impenitent transgressors of his law, wherever they may be. Hence Deborah sings:

"Jehovah, when thou wentest forth out of Seir,
When thou marchedst out of the field of Edom,
The earth trembled, the heavens also dropped,
Yea, the clouds dropped water,
The mountains quaked at the presence of Jehovah, . . ." (Judges 5:4, 5).

Similarly the picture of the wrath of God is associated with Edom, in Isa. 63:1, 3:
"Who is this that cometh from Edom?

Yea, I have trod them in mine anger
And trampled them in my wrath."

Moreover, the prophet Habakkuk prays:
"In wrath remember mercy,
God came from Teman,
And the Holy One from Mount Paran,

Before him went the pestilence,
And fiery bolts went forth at his feet."
(3:2, 3, 5).

From the above, it would seem, superficially, that the Edomites could not be forgiven. Yet, according to Deut. 23:8, they could enter the congregation of the Lord; and in the New Testament (Acts 15:17), they receive even greater blessings, as they are represented among those that become incorporated into the church. (Cf. Amos 9:12). The Edomites, therefore, represent a very striking antithesis to the Israel of God, but not, necessarily, a permanent antithesis. For the work of missions brings the remnant of Edom into the Israel of God, as we shall now see.

b. Patent spiritualization in N. T. Acts 15:17. We notice that in the New Testament this generalizing of the predicates of Edom reappears, in another form, but supporting the idea that this one enemy stands typically and spiritually for all the enemies of the Lord, and this virtually spiritualizes the concept of the enemies of the theocratic nation. For David's prophesied reign over the remnant of Edom, in Amos 9, is spiritualized into Christ's mediatorial kingship over the Gentile believers, by James, in Acts 15:17, where the military conquest makes room for the spiritual.

This is clear from the quotation of James, in Acts 15:16-18. He refers to the prophecy in Amos 9:11-12, concerning the Messiah's conquest of Edom, — *"that they may possess the remnant of Edom."*

Possessing the remnant of Edom is then spiritually understood by James, in that he sees illustrated, here, the purpose of God, *"that the residue of men may seek after the Lord."* (Acts 15:17).

Here the Holy Spirit endorses, through James, the practical import of His own prophecy, instead of giving the exact words, since this practical application of the Messiah's

How Would Christ Become King of Zion?

kingship over the Gentiles at large was the matter to be considered at Jerusalem.

We may, accordingly, be thankful that this Messianic kingship also includes us, if we belong to the remnant of man that seeks the Lord. Let us, therefore, look at the evidence, concerning the *manner* in which Christ's kingdom possesses the remnant of Edom, — in the words of James:

"And after they had held their peace, James answered, saying,

"Brethren, hearken unto me: Symeon hath rehearsed how first God visited the Gentiles, to take out of them a people for his name. And to this agree the words of the prophets; as it is written,

"After these things I will return,
And I will build the tabernacle of David, which is fallen;
And I will build again the ruins thereof,
And I will set it up:
That the residue of men may seek after the Lord,
(*Amos: "that they may possess the remnant of Edom,"*)
And all the Gentiles, upon whom my name is called,
Saith the Lord, who maketh these things known from of old."

(Acts 15:13-18, quoting Amos 9:11-12).

Two items are thus spiritually interpreted: *First, Edom: For where Amos has "the rem-*

nant of Edom," James makes use of the above interpretation of Edom and has "the residue of men."

Secondly, the physical conquest and possession of the enemies of God, by the Davidic dynasty, is spiritualized into their spiritual conquest and voluntary obedience unto the Messiah.

Now the figure of military conquest and possession is here used by Amos, possession "as in the days of old," (Amos 9:11), when David himself had conquered Edom by physical weapons. But, in a higher sense, the great Son of David, Jesus Christ, will possess the remnant of Edom and of mankind, at large.

Thus, where Amos has the figurative language of a military possessing of Edom by the dynasty of David, James shows what this figurative, military language really points forward to: "that the residue of men may seek after the Lord." It points to their spiritual conquest and voluntary allegiance to their Lord Jesus Christ.

Meanwhile the Edomites would be subjugated by the Messiah, because typical of all the enemies of the Messiah, and from that number some would come to rally loyally to his standard, though the others would meet with His just condemnation.[1]

---

[1] Many versions and recensions read "remnant of Edom." It is true that the Septuagint, and some manuscripts of the Syriac, read "remnant of man" (adam), instead. But this latter reading is readily explained, as one that would appeal to these translators as the easier one. However, the reading that is more difficult, for the translator, usually has more likelihood to have been the original. For translators are prone to simplify. Here then the more difficult reading, "remnant of Edom," has the preference. Moreover, the Old Testament never speaks of the "remnant of man" elsewhere, but in such connections it has the remnant of one or more nations. This usage would also favor "remnant of Edom," as the Hebrew

8. *The Cultus or Sacrificial System.* Again there is a spiritualization of the sacrificial system latent in the Old Testament, and evident in the New.

   a. Spiritualization of the Ark. Jer. 3:16. This applies to as central a feature of the cultus as the ark of the covenant. It will not function forever, but the time will come when it will have served its dispensational purpose, as is more than clear from Jer. 3:16. "And it shall come to pass, when ye are multiplied and increased in the land, in those days, saith Jehovah, neither shall it come to mind; neither shall they remember it; neither shall they miss it; neither shall it be made anymore."

   b. The Temple. Ezek. 40-47; Hebrews 9; 2 Cor. 6:16; I Peter 2:5. The Temple of Ezekiel has neither the Ark of the testimony, nor veil, suggesting that the time will come when they shall have served their typical task.

   This interpretation of Ezekiel's vision of the temple is reinforced when we contemplate the fact that the veil of the temple was rent in twain at Jesus' death. It also is strengthened when we consider that Heb. 9 spiritualizes the Holy of Holies, which the High Priest entered

---

original. However, the unauthoritative spiritualization of Edom, in the Septuagint, receives authoritative support, as the correct interpretation, in the above New Testament quotation of James. Thus the Holy Spirit gives an infallible interpretation of His own figurative language, in Amos 9, quoting from the Septuagint. To the textual student, it is evident that the Septuagint looked upon Edom as adam (man), and upon yarash (possess) as darash (seek), meanwhile completing the sense in its usual free but intuitive and brilliant manner! Yet this particular interpretation could be owned by the Spirit, as the practical import of the prophecy, and, therefore, as the infallible truth intended to be conveyed, — the Holy Spirit having, naturally, the right to interpret his own inspired prophecy, in a "spiritual" manner.

once a year not without blood, (verse 7), to be sprinkled upon the mercy-seat of the ark, and applies the symbolism to Christ, who entered the heaven of heavens with his own blood. Again, this spiritual interpretation of Ezekiel's temple is strengthened by the spiritualization of the temple in 2 Cor. 6:16: "And what agreement hath the temple of God with idols, for we are a temple of the living God, even as God said, I will dwell in them and walk in them." Paul here appeals to a latent spiritualization of the temple in the O. T., Lev. 26:12, And I will walk among you, and will be your God. Again, Peter considers his readers a spiritual house, I Peter 2:5. In the new heaven and new earth, the tabernacle of God is with men, Rev. 21:1-3, and the imagery of Ezekiel 47 in large part reappears, Rev. 22:1-5.

c. The Sacrifices. Ps. 107:22; Ps. 141:2; Ps. 51:17; Hos. 14:2; Isa. 19:23; I Sam. 15:22; Hos. 6:6; I Cor. 5:7; I Peter 2:4; John 4:20-24; Heb. 13:14, 15, 16. There is certainly also a measure of spiritualization of sacrifices, in various Old Testament passages. Prayer is regarded as incense in Psalm 141:2, "Let my prayer be set forth as incense before thee, and the lifting up of my hands as the evening sacrifices." Not only is prayer equated with sacrifices, but conversely sacrifices are also equated with prayer, — Ps. 107:22, "And let them offer the sacrifices of thanksgiving," Ps. 51:17, "The sacrifices of God are a broken spirit;" Hosea 14:2, "So will we render (as) bullocks (the offerings of) our lips;" similarly sacrifices stand over against vows, in a parallelism of Is. 19:23; "The Egyptians shall worship with sacrifice and oblation, and shall vow a vow unto Jehovah and shall perform it." If this is intended as a synonymous parallelism, then the sacrifices and the vows are spiritually identical.

Moreover, the Old Testament regards physical sacrifices as greatly inferior to the spiritual, I Sam. 15:22, "Hath Jehovah as great delight in burnt offering and sacrifices as in obeying the voice of Jehovah;" Hos. 6:6, "For I desire goodness and not sacrifice, and the knowledge of God, more than burnt-offering."

This latent spiritualization of sacrifices in the Old Testament is reinforced by the New Testament interpretation of sacrifices, in the New Testament eschatological state. I Cor. 5:7, "For our passover also hath been sacrificed, even Christ." "Christ gave himself up for us, an offering and a sacrifice to God, for an odor of sweet smell." Meanwhile Peter also considers his readers an "Holy priesthood, to offer up spiritual sacrifices, acceptable to God, through Jesus Christ." I Peter 2:4. And so the whole theocratic cultus receives a New Testament spiritual interpretation, reinforcing that adumbrated in the Old.

Thus the Messiah annuls the sacrificial system by his great sacrifice, our offerings are no longer bloody sacrifices.

9. *The Priestly, Royal and Prophetic Types.* — A part of the treatment of this subject has been covered elsewhere, and is, therefore, excluded here. For the prophecies dealing with the O. T. prophetic, priestly and royal *types of Christ have been surveyed*, in Chapters IV, V, and VI.

Moreover, the exclusively literal interpretation of these prophecies has been shown to lead to many difficulties and contradictions. These contradictions show how heavily burdened with difficulties is the Premillennial interpretation of the prophecies, dealing with Christ's predicted kingship of Jerusalem. (Cf. Chapter VII).

On the other hand, the Scripturally attested fulfillments of these prophecies are shown, in many instances, to support their "spiritual" interpretation, *as they apply to Christ*. These fulfillments show how Christ did become king of Jerusalem. (Cf. Chapter IX).

However, not only Christ, but *also his church is typified, in the Old Testament, with respect to its priestly, royal and prophetic tasks*. This involves the spiritual interpretation of the prophetic, priestly and royal types fulfilled in the church.

Let us, therefore, note some of the Biblical materials that illustrate and support the spiritualization that thus arises.

a. *The Spiritual Interpretation of the Priesthood as a Type of the Church.* —

1. Incipient Spiritualization in the O. T.: According to Exod. 19:6, all Israel may have the privilege of being a *priesthood:* "And

ye shall be unto me a kingdom of *priests* and a holy nation."

But the time will come that the priestly work of bringing (spiritual) sacrifices shall be carried out among *all nations*. "For from the rising of the sun, even unto the going down of the same, my name shall be great *among the Gentiles;* and in every place incense shall be offered unto my name, and *a pure offering:* for my name shall be great among the Gentiles, saith Jehovah of hosts." Malachi 1:11.[1]

2. More Complete Application of Priestly Characteristics to the Church, in the N. T.: The above quoted passage, from Exod. 19:6, is evidently referred to by Peter, when he says, "But ye are an elect race, a royal *priesthood*, a holy nation." 1 Peter 2:9.

The purpose of this priesthood is to bring *spiritual* offerings, — "to be *a holy priesthood, to offer up spiritual sacrifices,* acceptable to God through Jesus Christ." 1 Peter 2:4.

Priestly privileges are also extended "to the seven *churches* that are in Asia" (Rev. 1:4), for John says, "And he (Christ) made us to be a kingdom, to be *priests* unto his God and Father." Rev. 1:6.

Out of every nation, Christ purchased himself a priesthood. Hence they sing a

---
[1] Various other pre-exilic prophecies, concerning the priesthood, are, however, applicable to the O.T. post-exilic era. Evidently some or all of the following passages must be so interpreted: Jer. 33:17, 18; Ezek. 44:9-15; Ezek. 45:17; Mal. 2:4, 5.

new song, saying, "Worthy art thou to take the book, and to open the seals thereof: for thou wast slain, and didst purchase unto God with thy blood men *of every* tribe, and tongue, and people, and *nation*, and madest them to be unto our God a kingdom and *priests* . . ." Rev. 5:9, 10.

b. *The Spiritual Interpretation of Royalty as Typical of the Church.*

1. Incipient Spiritualization in the O. T.: As is evident from the foregoing, Israel may also have the privilege of being a kingdom: "And ye shall be unto me a *kingdom* of priests." (Ex. 19:6). The implications are developed in the N. T.

2. More Complete Application of Royal Characteristics to the Church, in the N. T.: Not only does Peter consider the church "a *royal* priesthood" (1 Peter 2:9), but even Christ says "to the angel of the *church in Laodicea*": "He that overcometh, *I will give to him to sit down with me in my throne*, as I also overcame, and sat down with my Father in his throne." Rev. 3:21.

However, not only in heaven, but also *on earth*, shall the church, saved out of *every nation*, reign: "For thou wast slain, and didst purchase unto God with thy blood men of *every . . . nation, . . . and they shall reign upon earth.*" Rev. 5: 9, 10.

To all eternity shall "they that have washed their robes" (Rev. 22:14) rule, for *"they shall reign for ever and ever."* (Rev. 22:5). This message comes to the church, for says our Lord: "I, Jesus, have sent mine angel to testify unto you these things for *the churches.*" Rev. 22:16.

c. *The Spiritual Interpretation of the Prophets as Typical of the church.*

1. Incipient Spiritualization in the O. T.: The great Pentecostal prophecy of Joel predicts the outpouring of the Holy Spirit upon the Church, in such a manner that its sons and daughters would prophesy: "And it shall come to pass afterward, that *I will pour out my Spirit upon all flesh; and your sons and your daughters shall prophesy, your old men shall dream dreams, your young men shall see visions;* and also upon the servants and upon the handmaids in those days will I pour out my Spirit." Joel 2:28, 29.

Not only the individual prophets, but Israel itself was called to be a light-bearer, in the O. T., — "Arise, shine; for thy light is come, and the glory of Jehovah is risen upon thee." (Isa. 60:1). — "Ye are my witnesses." (Isa. 43:10).—Compare Isa. 58:8, 10, where the light also involves good works. Furthermore, the dimly-burning, flaxen wick shall not be quenched. (Isa. 42:3) — Indeed, Jehovah will even provide "a light to the Gentiles." (Isa. 42:6).

He, too, promises that He will maintain the light on the "candlestick . . . Not by might, nor by power, but by my Spirit, saith Jehovah of hosts." (Zech. 4:1-6). "The general interpretation is that the golden candlestick represents the church."[1]

2. More Complete Application of Prophetic Characteristics to the Church, in the N. T.: To begin with this subordinate item of evidence, let us take up the N. T. evidence, *touching the candlestick,* immediately. Not only does Christ say, *"The seven candlesticks are seven churches."* (Rev. 1:20). But he also counsels his disciples, "Let your ... lamps be burning." (Luke 12:35). And Paul exhorts: "Do all things without murmurings, ... in the midst of a crooked and perverse generation, ... as lights in the world." (Phil. 2:14, 15).

But most clearly do we see the application of the prophetic characteristics to the church, in Peter's Pentecostal discourse. Though Joel had spoken of sons and daughters prophesying, Peter even explicitly includes the servants and the handmaidens of the Lord among those that shall prophesy, when he says: "But this is that which hath been spoken through the prophet Joel:

And it shall be in the last days, saith God, I will pour forth of my Spirit upon all flesh;

---

[1] Thus says Gaebelein, in his "Studies in Zechariah," page 44. It is positively refreshing to see how vainly Gaebelein attempts to escape the conclusion of the spiritual identity of Israel with the church, in his remarks concerning the typology of the candlestick, here.

How Would Christ Become King of Zion? 121

> *And your sons and your daughters shall prophesy,*
> And your young men shall see visions,
> And your old men shall dream dreams:
> *Yea and on my servants and on my handmaidens in those day*
> *Will I pour forth of my Spirit; and they shall prophesy."* (Acts 2:16-18).

Certainly Peter's great Pentecostal discourse applies prophetic characteristics to the church as much as Jesus' spiritual interpretation of the candlestick: "The seven candlesticks are the seven churches."[1]

10. *The Covenant of Grace.* This covenant is broad and comprehensive, and includes elements that have been treated above. Moreover, it is fundamental to all Jehovah's later covenantal dealings.

But the main question, now before us, is evidently this: What is the Biblical teaching concerning *"the new covenant,"* which Scripture contrasts with the old?

The character of *the old covenant* is shown especially in Ex. 19:5, 6 — "Now, therefore, if ye will . . . keep my *covenant*, . . . ye shall be unto me a *kingdom* of priests and a holy nation." This covenant Israel accepted, *as a nation*, at Sinai.

Here it is the old covenant that results in the typical, theocratic kingdom of God. The future

---

[1] As the typology of the candlestick was brought in here, in a subordinate way, so various other subsidiary, typical items might have been treated, in this chapter, in dealing with other leading features of the typical kingdom. But it would seem somewhat unnecessary, to the argument, to treat additional, 'subordinate, typical items.

of this old covenant is, therefore, bound up with the future of this typical kingdom; and it is the future of this kingdom that interests us.

How then is this old covenant spiritualized, according to the Biblical teaching concerning the new covenant? And what is the relation of both the new covenant, and of this old covenant, to the covenant of grace made with Abraham? These questions will now be taken up.

Meanwhile, these inquiries are also fundamental to the questions whether infant baptism should be rejected or not, and whether the moral law should still have a place in our public worship. *How then do the Scriptures contrast the new covenant and the old?*

a. *Latent Spiritual Interpretation of the Old Covenant in the Old Testament Scriptures.* — Though Isaiah and Hosea refer to this old, national, Sinaitic covenant, its spiritualization comes to the fore especially in Jeremiah 31:31-34: "Behold the days come, saith Jehovah, that I will make a *new covenant* with the house of Israel and with the house of Judah: 32 *not according to the covenant that I made with their fathers in the day that I took them by the hand to bring them out of the land of Egypt;* which my covenant they break, although I was a husband unto them, saith Jehovah. 33. But this is the covenant that I will make with the house of Israel, after those days saith Jehovah: I will put my law in their inward parts, and in their heart will I write it; and I will be their God, and they shall be my people. 34. And they shall teach no more every man his neighbor and every man his brother, saying, know Jehovah: for they shall all know me, from the least of them unto the greatest of them, saith Jehovah: for I will forgive their iniquity, and their sin will remember no more."

It is clear that the new covenant is here contrasted with the old, Sinaitic covenant, *when the Lord brought their fathers out of the land of Egypt.* It is to be noticed that the new covenant is here *not* contrasted with the Abrahamic covenant. This is an item, of Biblical evidence, of far reaching importance, as we shall see now in connection with Hebrews 8:13, which treats of the end of the old covenant, indeed, it was "nigh unto vanishing away." But the covenant with Abraham is not said to be ended, nor did it vanish away, nor is the term "old covenant" ever applied to the Abrahamic covenant, by the Scriptures.

The chief differences between the Abrahamic and the Sinaitic covenants will come up, after the treatment of the New Testament texts referring to the new covenant. These will now be cited.

b. *Evident Spiritual Interpretation of the Old Covenant in the New Testament Scriptures.*

The above section from Jer. 31:31-34 is quoted, substantially, in Hebrews 8:8-12. The reference to the Sinaitic covenant is retained in verses 8 and 9: "Behold, the days come, saith the Lord, that I will make a new covenant with the house of Israel and with the house of Judah; not according to the covenant that I made with their fathers, *In the day that I took them by the hand to lead them forth out of the land of Egypt...*"

Here, again, the new covenant is contrasted with Sinaitic, *as the old covenant*. For it was the Sinaitic covenant that was made, *when the Lord led Israel forth out of the land of Egypt,* while the Abrahamic covenant had been made 430 years earlier, according to Gal. 3:17.[1]

Of this Sinaitic covenant, but not of the Abrahamic covenant, it is therefore said in Hebrews 8:13, "In that he saith, a new covenant, he hath made the first old; but that which is becoming old and waxeth aged is nigh unto vanishing away." The sacrificial system of the Sinaitic covenant did vanish with the destruction of the temple in 70 A.D., and had really been fulfilled long before. Thus the Sinaitic superstructure became antiquated. But its foundation, the Abrahamic covenant, was never abrogated, and still stands today, as the abiding basis of the new superstructure, the new covenant.

Again, in 2 Cor. 3:6, "the new covenant" is contrasted with the Sinaitic, as the old covenant, and not with the Abrahamic covenant. For in the Sinaitic covenant, the law was written on "tables of stone," verse 3, but in

---

[1] Compare the Greek (Septuagintal) translation of Ex. 12:40; and C. R. Conder's splendid article, on the "Exodus," in the International Standard Bible Encyclopaedia.

"the new covenant" it is written "in tables that are hearts of flesh." The prophecy here quoted, foretelling that the law would be written in the heart, refers to Jer. 31:33, as Hebrews 8:10 had also referred to the same prophecy. This writing of the law in our hearts is a long process, and even with the reading of the law every Lord's day, in public worship, the process of the Spirit's writing the law in the hearts is not completed in this life. How unscriptural, therefore, to set aside the reading of the law in public worship! Instead, one should appreciate the work of the Spirit, as he writes this law in the heart, by blessing its regular reading. Accordingly, one should meditate much on the law in order that it may be written ever more deeply in the heart.

Moreover, the light of the foregoing Biblical usage of "the new covenant," as contrasted with the old covenant, is necessary to interpret the words of our Lord: "This cup is *the new covenant* in my blood" (Luke 22:20, 1 Cor. 11:25). Thus, evidently, the blood of the new covenant is here implicitly contrasted with the blood of the old, Sinaitic covenant. This contrast points to the ceremony of Ex. 24:6-8, that took place at Sinai, where first the altar and then Israel were sprinkled with the blood of an animal sacrifice, — while the new covenant is established in the atoning blood of Christ (Hebrews 9:19, 20).

c. *Summary of the Spiritual Interpretation of the Old, Sinaitic Covenant as Contrasted with the new Covenant.* — The covenant of grace, made with Abraham, is fundamental to both the new covenant and to the old, Sinaitic covenant, with which Scripture contrasts this new covenant. As therefore the old Sinaitic covenant was built upon the abiding foundation of the covenant with Abraham (Gal. 3:15-17), so also the new covenant was built upon this same abiding basis. And, as the old, Sinaitic covenant represented the first superstructure upon this eternal foundation, so also the new covenant represented a new superstructure upon this same, abiding, basic covenant of grace, made with Abraham. Moreover, when the old Sinaitic covenant, as the old superstructure, had waxed aged and vanished away (Hebrews 8:13), the new covenant, as the new superstructure, took its place.

This new covenant may be contrasted with the old in several respects. Four points of contrast are here noted, in connection with the old covenant and the new. Thus the old superstructure, in four respects, which are comparable to the four walls of this superstructure, makes room for the new superstructure, or new covenant. Let us itemize first, then, four characteristic features of the new covenant, as the new superstructure, and follow these up with the four corresponding and contrasting features of the old superstructure, the old covenant.

Four items may be stressed in connection with the new covenant.

First: This is the new covenant in Christ's blood (Luke 22:20; 1 Cor. 11:25).

Secondly: The ethical law is written, by the Spirit, on the tables of the heart. (Jer. 31:33; 2 Cor. 3:3; Hebrews 8:10).

Thirdly: Christ, our great High Priest, has brought his sacrifice (Heb. 8:3), and there is no more offering for sin. (Heb. 10:18).

Fourthly: The Israel with whom this covenant was made (Heb. 8:10), is the Israel after the Spirit, including Jews, as branches that remained in the olive tree or were restored, and including Gentiles that were grafted into the same olive tree (Rom. 11:17-24; Eph. 2:12, 19; Rev. 21:9, 12).

Correspondingly, four matters may also be emphasized, in connection with the old, Sinaitic covenant, made when Jehovah led Israel forth out of the land of Egypt, (Jer. 31:32; Heb. 8:9; 2 Cor. 3:7).

First: This was the old covenant, in the blood of a mere animal sacrifice, — whose *blood was sprinkled first on the altar, then on the people,* typifying both justification and the sanctified spiritual life (Ex. 24:6-8; Hebrews 9:19, 20).

Secondly: The ethical law was written *on tables of stone*. When Paul contrasts these stone tables with the characteristics of the "new covenant" (2 Cor. 3:6), he says, ". . . ye are . . . written . . . *not in tables of stone,* but in tables that are hearts of flesh" (verse 3). The stone tables contained the Sinaitic moral law.

However, some safeguarding statements are surely in order here. Paul does not mean that we have nothing to do with the moral law. For this moral law, itself, must evidently still be written "in tables that are hearts of flesh," and this law is, therefore, still normative for the church. The progressive writing of the moral law, "in tables that are hearts of flesh," must therefore continue from Lord's Day to Lord's Day, and hence the moral law should be regularly read, in the public worship of the church.

But this moral law, itself, must be distinguished here, from the "tables of stone," on which it was written in the Sinaitic covenant. How is this applied here by Paul?

Some of the Jews, "corrupting the word of God" (2 Cor. 2:17), refuse to accept Christ, and prefer the law, instead. However, to them the law written "in tables of stone," and not "in tables that are hearts of flesh," represents a "the ministration of death" (verse 7), and "the ministration of condemnation" (verse 9), for "the letter killeth" (verse 6).

But to those that accept Christ, "the spirit giveth life" (verse 6). To them the law is, accordingly, included, in "the ministration of the spirit" (verse 8), and "the ministration of righteousness" (verse 9).

How Would Christ Become King of Zion? 129

Meanwhile, though there was also gospel in the law, yet those refusing the gospel find in the law that "the letter killeth" (verse 6), while those accepting the gospel in the law experience that "the spirit giveth life" (verse 6).

Hence those that desire falsely to exalt the old Sinaitic covenant, by ignoring the "new covenant" (verse 6), serve the letter that killeth; while Paul teaches that he and his associates are "ministers of a new covenant" (verse 6), and hence of the spirit that giveth life (verse 6), so that the law is written in tables that are hearts of flesh.

Paul is here, therefore, not directly contrasting the new covenant with the old Sinaitic covenant, as it should have been interpreted, by the Jews of his day, for then they would have seen gospel even in the law.

But Paul here contrasts the "new covenant" with the old Sinaitic covenant, as it was actually misinterpreted by the self-righteous Jews of his day, so as to exclude the gospel.

Yet when Paul speaks of a new covenant here, he is using the well-known words of the prophecy of Jeremiah 31:31, and the words of Christ in Luke 22:20. Now the new covenant is described by Jeremiah, as more inward than the old, "I will put my law in their inward parts, and in their heart will I write it" (31:33). This represents a contrast with the old Sinaitic covenant (31:32), which was somewhat more outward, even in the day that

Jehovah took their fathers "by the hand to bring them out of the land of Egypt" (31:32), unto Mount Sinai.

This more outward character of the old Sinaitic covenant is therefore symbolized by the tables of stone that have disappeared, while the more inward character of the new covenant is indicated by the fact that the law is here said to be written in tables that are hearts of flesh. This makes the moral law not less normative under the new covenant than the old. But, on the contrary, it works precisely the other way. It even makes the moral law more deeply binding upon the church, because it is written more deeply in the hearts of those of the new covenant.

Thirdly: The priests administered the sacrificial system which had waxed aged and was nigh unto vanishing away (Hebrews 8:13), because of Christ's great sacrifice.

Fourthly: The Israel with whom this covenant was made was the Israel that the Lord had just led forth from Egypt (Jer. 31:32), and that received at Sinai *a body of civil laws intended especially for Israel's national life,* until the time of the new covenant, which was to include Hebrews and Corinthians alike (Heb. 8; 2 Cor. 3), under various systems of civil laws. Thus we see that in four respects the old, Sinaitic superstructure made room for the new superstructure of the new covenant.

d. *The Covenant with Abraham, as the Abiding Foundation, first of the Old, Sinaitic Covenant, and then of the New Covenant.* — This covenant with Abraham, being basic, to both the old Sinaitic covenant and the new covenant, is stressed in Hebrews and elsewhere in its eternal, unchangeable respects. The interpretation that the Holy Spirit, therefore, gives to this covenant is predominantly concerned with its eternity, though some of the elements have meanwhile undergone a spiritualization that enlarges their meaning. For the sake of brevity only a few matters are here pointed out in connection with this Abrahamic covenant as the basis, especially, of the new covenant.

First: It is a covenant of *grace*. "Abraham believed God and it was reckoned unto him for righteousness" (Gal. 3:6-17; Gen. 15:6). Not only the old Sinaitic covenant (Gal. 3:15-17, but also the new covenant is founded on this eternal mercy of God, for Jehovah says, explicitly, that he also bases the new covenant on his mercy: "For I will be merciful to their iniquities and their sins will I remember no more." (Hebrew 8:12; Jer. 31:34).

Secondly: This covenant includes the *believers and their children, as the people of the Lord.* God promises Abraham "to be a God unto thee *and to thy seed after thee*" (Gen. 17:7). This promise looms up in the background of Acts 2:39. "For to you is the promise *and to you children.*" It comes more to the foreground in 1 Cor. 7:14, "Else were *your children* unclean; but now they *are holy.*" Hence circumcision, as spiritually interpreted, signifies the same as baptism (Col. 2:11, 12): "In whom ye were also circumcised with the circumcision not made with hands, in the putting off of the body of the flesh, in the circumcision of Christ; having been buried with him in baptism, wherein ye were also raised with him through faith in the working of God, who raised him from the dead." This shows that adult baptism signifies the same as the circumcision of the heart. Paul could never say that, if baptism had not taken the place of circumcision. But as circumcision was applied to adults or to children, according to the circumstances, so also there is adult baptism as well as infant baptism. Both "baptisms" are fundamental, because they belong to the "foundation of repentance from dead works, and of faith toward God, and *of teaching of baptisms* and of the laying of hands, and of resurrection of the dead and of eternal judgment" (Hebrews 6: 1, 2). These are among "the first principles of Christ" (Hebrews 6:1), to be considered elemental and of primary importance.

Jehovah's promise that he will be a God to Abraham *and his seed* (Gen. 17:7), is also implied in Heb. 8:10, "And I will be to them a God and they shall be to me a people." This promise is mentioned in connection with the new covenant, in Heb. 8:10. As then the covenant people, in Abraham's day, included the seed of the covenant, so God is the God of his people, also in the new covenant, to this day.

Thirdly: This covenant with Abraham is *unchangeable*, — "immutable" (Heb. 6:17, 18) — in its promise concerning the children. It is this very subject of the seed of the covenant that is brought into connection with the unchangeable character of this covenant, in Heb. 6:13-17. Though certain forms, such as the sacraments may change, the essence of the covenant remains immutable. Its immutable character is emphasized, not only by the oath of the covenant to Abraham in Gen. 22:16, but this oath is again stressed in Heb. 6:13-17, for the reassurance of those in the new covenant that this new covenant has an "immutable," unchangeable foundation.

Fourthly: Abraham and his seed are made *heirs*, not only of the ancient holy land (Gen. 15:18), but Paul regards Abraham as "heir of the *world*" (Rom. 4:13). Peter speaks of "an inheritance incorruptible, and undefiled, and that fadeth not away, reserved in *heaven* for you" (1 Peter 1:4, 5). Christ tells us that the meek "shall inherit the earth" (Mat. 5:5).

Thus the inheritance comes to include not only the ancient Holy Land, but much more besides. It has now been interpreted to include "the world" (Rom. 4:13), even "heaven" (1 Peter 4), and "earth" (Mat. 5:5); the kingdom" (1 Cor. 6:9; 15:50; Eph. 5:5); "eternal life" (Titus 3:7). Similarly Hebrews speaks of "the eternal inheritance" (9:15). Clearly, Israel's heritage was not understood as the mere land of Canaan, by Jehovah who promised it, nor even by Abraham, to whom it was promised. For we read of "the city which hath foundations, whose builder and maker is God," as the chief attraction, to Abraham, of "the inheritance" (Heb. 11:8), to which he looked forward, according to the promises.

As children of the covenant and therefore as heirs, we also look forward, confidently, to the same "eternal inheritance."[1]

11. *The O. T. Sacraments:*

a. Circumcision:
1. Latent spiritualization in the O. T.: Deut. 10:16; 30:6; Jer. 4:4. The Old Testament sacraments are, finally, also spiritualized. The latent spiritualization of circumcision is clear, Deut. 10:16; 30:6, "And Jehovah thy God will circumcise thy heart, and the heart of thy seed, to love Jehovah thy God with all thy heart and with all thy soul, that thou mayest live." Compare Jer. 4:4; 6:10; 9:26.
2. Evident spiritualization in the N. T. Rom. 2:28. In the New Testament baptism takes

---

[1] The position is sometimes advanced that Jehovah made two covenants with Abraham, one involving the inheritance for Israel, and the other covenant involving spiritual blessings. But does Holy Writ afterwards speak thus of God's "covenants with Abraham?" Scarcely, — on the contrary, God's covenantal activities with Abraham are later unified and looked upon as the "covenant with Abraham," or the covenant made with Abraham, Isaac and Jacob, or with the patriarchs. Compare Ex. 2:24; 6:4-8; Deut. 7:9; 8:18; 9:5; 10:15; Luke 1:72; Acts 3:25.

the place of circumcision, and the latter is entirely spiritualized, Rom. 2:28, 29; 15:8; Phil. 3:3; Col. 2:11, 12; 3:11.

b. Passover:
1. Latent spiritualization in the O. T.: The sacrament of the passover was a sacrifice, and as such shares the spiritualization of all the sacrifices as that comes to the fore both in the Old Testament and in the New.
2. Evident spiritualization in the N. T.: I Cor. 5:7. Moreover the Passover was displaced by the Lord's Supper, as may be inferred from Matt. 26:26-28; Mark 14:12-15; Luke 22: 7-20. And the Passover, as far as the New Testament is concerned, is directly spiritualized in I Cor. 5:7, "For our passover also hath been sacrificed, even Christ."

Thus the sacraments of the O. T. cannot find a place in Christ's kingdom but God gives his covenant people their spiritual import and replaces them by sacraments that are appropriate to the N. T. day.

B. — THERE IS ESPECIALLY AN ORGANIC SPIRITUALIZATION OF OLD TESTAMENT SCRIPTURE

This Word was also an important element of the typical kingdom of God. For what would this kingdom have been without the Word?

The spiritual interpretation of these Scriptures, however, is concerned not only with individual items,[1] as shown above, under A, but it is emphatically *organic*, though the scope and limits of this spiritualization will be treated later, in Chapter X.

Since the individual elements, discussed above under A, are organically related, the organic spiritualization of Old Testament Scripture is the result. This is, naturally, concerned especially with Christ's predicted kingship, — in fact with all his Messianic work.

We now take up, then, the *organic* spiritualization of Old Testament Scripture, — *whether this Word was given to the covenant people through the law and the prophets, or sung, responsively, by the people, through the psalms.*

1. *The Psalter as the Praise-book of the Kingdom.* The Psalter becomes well nigh as significant, in the worship of the theocracy and of the church, as do the sacraments. But this praise-book of the kingdom also expresses and receives an organic spiritualization, in the worship of Jehovah's covenant people.

That the Psalter is here taken up, separately, among the Biblical books, is due to its unique place in the institutional life of the kingdom, in both the Old Testament and the New. It is due to its divinely ordained use, in public worship, in the Old Testament, without the abrogation of

---

[1] The method of studying individual, Biblical items, as used above, is occasioned, partly, by the fact that the discussion is exegetical, rather than dogmatic; but it also arises from the fact that this study aims to refute, in part, what has been called a "biblicistic" type of Premillennial literature. Cf. Dr. William H. Rutgers, "Premillennialism in America," pages 150-155; compare, for the term, "biblicistic," Dr. R. Bronkema, "The Essence of Puritanism," pages 80-124. However, the organic character of the spiritual interpretation of O.T. Scripture needs to be emphasized.

this use in the New, but rather its reinforcement, as a praise-book of the church, as well.

a. Incipient spiritualization in the O. T. use of the Psalter — There were various spiritualizations, in the Psalter, sung by ancient Israel — as of the inheritance of the saints (73:26; 16:5; 142:5, 119:57) and of their sacrifices of praise (107:22; 141:2; 51:17), and implicitly of the other elements of the theocracy.

But this spiritualization was voiced particularly, in the various, magnificent psalms that typified leading events in the life of our Lord Jesus Christ. These typical psalms are illustrated, in part, in the following typically-prophetic verses, whose collective content is intended to be understood as including the spiritualized exaltation of our Lord, — as is clear from the way in which the Holy Spirit gives these verses a spiritualized interpretation in their New Testament quotations[1]. The exaltation of our Lord, to which these verses lead, certainly does not require a Millennial earthly rule at Jerusalem. A far more spiritual rule is the climax of these verses:

118:22, The stone, which the builders rejected,
  Is become the head of the corner.
22:1, My God, my God, why hast thou forsaken me?
22:18, They parted my garments among them,
  And upon my vesture did they cast lots.

---

[1] These quotations are presented under b, of this section.

16:10, Thou wilt not leave my soul in Sheol,
Neither wilt thou suffer thy holy one
to see corruption.
68:18, Thou hast ascended on high, . . .
110:1, Jehovah said unto my Lord,
Sit thou at my right hand . . .

Thus the Psalter, especially in the prophetic psalms, as sung by the O. T. covenant people, voiced before Israel's consciousness, something of the future hope. This hope was expressed there by the Holy Spirit Himself, with an incipiently spiritualized intent, and with an organic unity, centering in the Messiah.

b. Evident Spiritualization in the New Testament use of the Psalter. — But the Psalter, in the prophetic hope that it expresses, is greatly illuminated and, therefore, still more clearly spiritualized, by the New Testament fulfillments concerned. These fulfillments clarify the meaning voiced by the psalms, as they are sung, in public worship, by the church, the kingdom of the new day.[1]

Let us, therefore, now take up, as examples, the above verses, just quoted, to indicate their New Testament fulfillments.

Thus Psalm 118:22 — "the stone which the builders rejected" — is fulfilled in Christ, according to Mat. 21:42; Mark 12:10; Luke 10:17; Acts 4:11; Eph. 20:20; 1 Pet. 2:7.

Of Psalm 22, as applying to Good Friday, verse 1 — "My God, my God, why hast thou

---

[1] The evidence for the spiritualization of the kingdom is given on page 94.

How Would Christ Become King of Zion? 139

forsaken me?" — is fulfilled in Mat. 27:46 and Mark 15:34; while verse 18 — "Upon my vesture did they cast lots" — is fulfilled in Mat. 27:35; Luke 23:24 and John 19:24.

As applying to the Easter theme of Christ's resurrection, Psalm 16:10 — "Thou wilt not leave my soul in Sheol . . ." is referred to as fulfilled, by Acts 13:35.

And, as pertaining to the Ascension of our Lord, Psalm 68:18 — "Thou hast ascended on high . . ." — is fulfilled according to Eph. 4:8; while Ps. 110:1, as predicting his sitting at the Father's right hand, is fulfilled, according to Mat. 22:44; Mark 12:36; Luke 20:42; Acts 2:34; Hebrews 1:13.[1] And in none of these places is any hope held out for the premillennial fulfillment of these prophecies, touching Christ's royal exaltation.

Thus the Psalter is shown to have an evident spiritualization in its New Testament quotations and fulfillments, concerned especially with the Christ.

It is clearly in this light that it is to be sung, in public worship, by the New Testament covenant people, because it is also intended to voice the subjective response of the church to these many prophecies, as spiritually fulfilled.

For it is, evidently, in this more spiritual way that the Holy Spirit intends the Psalter

---

[1] See page 159, where, according to Acts 2:30, 34, Christ's sitting on the throne of David is shown to be interpreted by Peter as equivalent to his sitting at the right hand of the Father.

to be understood by the church, when it uses this praise-book, in public worship.[1]

2. *The Old Testament Scriptures as They Treat of the Future of the Typical Kingdom.*

Word and sacraments go together. Not only do the Old Testament sacraments partake of the spiritualization shown,[2] but naturally the Old Testament Scriptures, themselves, contain and receive an organic spiritualization. Indeed, not only the Psalter, as the praise-book of the kingdom, but the entire Old Testament, as a canon of the kingdom, is thus affected.

Now this Old Testament Word of God is an even more important, vital, and abiding element of the typical kingdom than are the sacraments or the prophets, the kings and the priests of which it treats. For these sacraments, priests, kings and prophets have all disappeared, as they led up to the Christ and to their counterparts in the church.

But the Old Testament Scriptures were not alone a vital element of the theocracy, and they have not only led up to the New Testament Scriptures, they still serve as a rule of faith and practice for the church in the manner that the new Testament spiritualizes and applies them.

a. However, these Old Testament Scriptures, as they treated of the future of the typical kingdom, had to be understood, even in Old Testament times, in the light of the latent and incip-

---
[1] cf. the author's article on "The Psalms in Christian Liturgy," in the latest edition (1929) of **The International Standard Bible Encyclopedia**.
[2] See page 134.

ient spiritualizations they contain, as these concern the future of the kingdom of the Messiah.

They are so understood and interpreted by the Septuagintal translators, before Christ, in various prophetic passages. However, some of the Jewish Apocryphal writings did not take enough cognizance of this spiritualization.

b. But now, in New Testament times, these Old Testament Scriptures are naturally to be understood in the light of the clear and complete spiritualizations contained in the New Testament. For all the vital elements of theocracy treated above, as spiritualized, are to be understood in this spiritualized sense, in the Old Testament whenever these Scriptures treat of the future of the typical kingdom, in such a way as to apply also to the church of Christ.

For, on the one hand, the church continued, in spiritualized form, all the vital elements of the theocracy. And on the other hand, the church's history does not require the ancient Holy Land as its special locality, nor ancient Jerusalem as its capital, as of old.

Yet Jerusalem and the other geographical features of Palestine and of other Bible lands continue to exist, after the close of the theocracy, that is after Christ. These geographical features also have a history of their own, which may be in part predicted, in a very literal way.

Hence the great question arises, as to the

scope of the literal fulfillments of prophecy, and the scope of the spiritual fulfillments.

Before we take up this question, in Chapter X, let us summarize the results demonstrated thus far. They find their organic, unifying principle in the vital phases of the theocracy that abide, in the church, through their spiritualized counterparts.

And the theocracy is as central to the premillennial view, as it is to the following summary of the Biblical teaching, concerning the future of this typical kingdom.

The Scriptures then point us to the following spiritualizations that must be taken into consideration, in dealing with the future of the typical kingdom, and especially in interpreting texts that involve the future spiritualized form of this kingdom.

These spiritualizations are fundamental to the interpretive principles that are now to be unified and summarized.

C. — INTERPRETIVE PRINCIPLES THUS DERIVED FROM THE SCRIPTURES TO ILLUMINE THE PREDICTED KINGSHIP OF CHRIST

The main difficulty with the Premillennial positions, accordingly, lies in its leading interpretive principle, on which objection is made against spiritualizing various prophecies, while the Old Testament itself, supported by the New, suggests considerable scope for this very principle of spiritualization.

For, in an inductive way, we have shown that this

principle is recognized, latently in the O. T., and evidently in the New, with respect to all the more permanent elements of the theocratic kingdom, as these are given an eschatological significance.

Taking the fundamental principle of spiritualization, thus vouched for, we may, on the basis of the passages inductively studied, hold to the following more specific interpretive principles:

1. *The spiritualization of the capital of the theocratic kingdom, Zion, or Jerusalem;*
2. *The spiritualization of the Holy Land, the inheritance of the saints;*
3. *The spiritualization of the Kingdom;*
4. *The spiritualization of the Seed of Abraham;*
5. *The spiritualization of the Covenant-People, as the Bride of the Lord;*
6. *The spiritualization of Israel;*
7. *The spiritualization of Israel's enemies, as typified in the Edomites;*
8. *The spiritualization of the physical conquest of the enemies of the theocracy into their spiritual conquest, and voluntary obedience, as similarly typified in the case of Edom;*
9. *The spiritualization of the Temple;*
10. *The spiritualization of the Sacrifices;*
11. *The spiritual interpretation of the Priestly, Royal and Prophetic Types;*
12. *The spiritualization of the Old Covenant;*
13. *The spiritualization of Circumcision;*
14. *The spiritualization of the Passover;*

15. *The organic spiritualization of the Psalter, as the Praise-book of the kingdom;*
16. *The organic spiritualization of the Old Testament Scriptures, as they treat of the future of the kingdom;*
17. *The more latent spiritualization of these theocratic elements in the Old Testament and their more evident spiritualization in the New;*
18. *The incipient application of this spiritualization to the theocratic kingdom itself, the fuller application to the eschatological kingdom.*

We have seen the Biblical evidence for the spiritualization of every vital element of the theocracy. Now all these spiritualizations evidently point to the manner in which Christ would become King of Jerusalem.

D. — HOW THEN WOULD CHRIST BECOME KING?

Many prophecies imply some kind of Messianic reign of Christ over Zion, premillennial or otherwise. Let us consider his prophesied kingship, in connection with Jerusalem, the Promised Land, and Israel, for these three items are of central importance, in any case.

1. *How Christ would, therefore, be King of Jerusalem.*

Since Jerusalem is generalized, as we have seen above,[1] by Isaiah (49:14; 51:3; 52:1), to include every locality where exiled Israel would be scattered, it is natural to conclude that Christ would be king

---
1) cf. Pages 88-91.

wherever his dispersed true Zion would be found. Even though there should be an increasing return of the Jews to Jerusalem and a general conversion of those in Palestine, Zion, as used by Isaiah, would still include all true sons of Zion, throughout the world.

Furthermore, since we also saw that the Jerusalem which is above, Gal. 4:26, is representative of God's people in heaven, it is clear that such a spiritualization of Jerusalem points to a heavenly kingship of Christ over his people in the church triumphant above.

Moreover, since the spiritual Zion to which the Christians have come, according to Hebrews 12:12, represents the church on earth, the implication is natural that Christ would become king of this spiritual Zion, the church militant, including naturally its manifestations in Jerusalem, but also extending unto the uttermost parts of the earth.

Finally, since the New Jerusalem coming down from heaven[1] is clearly identified with the bride of the Lamb,[2] namely the church, the implication is clear that Christ's kingship over this Jerusalem coming down from heaven is identical with his kingship over his glorified church. This church will be glorified in the new heaven and new earth. Then, too, the New Jerusalem will come down from heaven.

Now in all the above different usages of Jerusalem or Zion, as spiritualized, there is evidently an organic unity. For they all, in their present day appli-

---
1) cf. Rev. 21:10.
2) cf. Rev. 21:9.

cation, concern the church, though from different points of view.

Hence the manner in which Christ would become king of Jerusalem or Zion is identical with the way in which he would become king of his church.

Of course there may here also be found literally fulfilled details, which derive their main significance from their relationship to this spiritual interpretation, in an organic way.

But if the prophecies of Christ's kingship over Zion are not fulfilled in any more literal way than suggested above, we will still have to admit that the prophecy was *fulfilled,* in the spiritual manner thus permitted by the Scriptural spiritualizations of Zion.

In fact this spiritual fulfillment is not only permitted by the Scriptures. It is required by the sumtotal of the above spiritualizations, centering in the Old Testament theocracy, and in its New Testament counterpart, the church.

That Christ thus actually became king of his spiritual Zion, in fulfillment of the prophecies, according to the New Testament, we shall see in Chapter IX.

Hence the expectation that Christ will be king of Jerusalem, in a literal way, during the Millennium, lacks all Scriptural necessity.

That God, meanwhile, remains free to fulfill the prophecies more literally than the Scriptures themselves require, cannot be denied in the abstract.

But the premillennial view lacks all solid Scriptural necessity and foundation here, and has in its historical development encountered the many contradictions cited in Chapter VII.

Hence we conclude that Christ would be king of Zion — of Jerusalem — in the manner supported by the above spiritualizations of Zion and Jerusalem. In other words, he would thus be king of his church, militant and triumphant, temporal and external, — world-wide in its scope.

2. *How Christ would be King of the Promised Land.*

Now let us pursue the present question, how Christ would become king of Jerusalem, a bit further. It clearly is closely related to the similar question, how Christ would become king of the holy land, the inheritance of the promised seed of Abraham.

And the foregoing generalizations and spiritualizations of this inheritance,[1] again point to the manner of Christ's predicted kingship over the once holy land, the inheritance of the faithful children of Israel.

For if the meek shall *inherit* not only the promised land but *the earth,* Mat. 5:5, how does that affect their king, Jesus Christ, who also came meek and lowly?[2] Shall he not continue to be their king when they inherit the earth? Hence he shall reign not only over the promised land, but over his people, as they inherit the very earth.

Again, though Abraham was of old, to be heir of the holy land of promise, does not Paul's generalizing statement, that Abraham would be *heir of the world,*[3] imply something with respect to Christ's kingship? For Christ reigns over the children of

---
1) cf. Page 91.
2) cf. Mat. 21:5.
3) Rom. 4:13.

Abraham, wherever they are in the world. Hence again Christ's kingship is to be associated with an Abrahamitic inheritance that will not only include Canaan, but that will be world-wide.

This is all the more clear because of the fact that the inheritance of Abraham's seed is made dependent upon their attitude to Christ, in Gal. 3:29, "And if ye are Christ's, then are ye Abraham's seed, heirs according to the promise." The heirship to the promise of old included Canaan, but it evidently includes here, as in Romans 4:13, "the world." Hence again we come to the conclusion that Christ's kingship of the promised land must be understood in the light of the enlarged inheritance of Abraham's seed, who with Abraham are heirs "of the world."

Meanwhile, when Hebrews 9:15 speaks of an *eternal inheritance,* there is again an implication with respect to Christ's kingship. For when his people receive their eternal inheritance, he will still be their king. He will therefore be king of a people whose inheritance is not only world-wide, but also eternal. Far from merely inheriting Palestine, his people will be eternal heirs of the world, with him as their glorified king. If ye are Christ's, then, are ye Abraham's seed, heirs of the enlarged, eternal and glorified inheritance, under Christ your eternal king.

Even Peter, who stood close to the Jews, points in the same direction. When he begins his first letter, he does not develop the hope of Christ's Millennial reign over Palestine, though he treats of the future hope. He, himself, was a Jew, and includes himself

How Would Christ Become King of Zion? 149

in "a living hope."[1] But this hope is here, on the one hand, not expressly limited to Canaan, at any time in the future. On the other hand, Peter uses the concept of the inheritance, associated from of old with Palestine, but he connects this idea of the inheritance with the heavenly salvation, ready to be revealed in the last time. And so he points to the hope of *"an inheritance, incorruptible, and undefiled, and that fadeth not away, reserved in heaven for you, . . . a salvation ready to be revealed in the last time."*

Here again we come to the conclusion that the inheritance of the Saints, Jewish and Gentile, when revealed in the last time, will include the new heaven and the new earth. Over these Gentile and Jewish saints, Christ will reign. But though his rule does not exclude the ancient Palestine, it extends wherever his people is found, throughout their world-wide, eternal inheritance, of the new heaven and new earth.

And so again the expectation that Christ will be king of Palestine, in a literal fashion, during the Millennium, lacks all Scriptural necessity.

Hence one must hold that the prophecies concerned have been fulfilled, even if they are fulfilled only in the above spiritualized fashion.

They will be fulfilled in this spiritualized fashion, even if they should also be fulfilled literally, in this instance.

Hence the spiritual interpretation is true, in any case.

And the literal interpretation, as historically de-

---
[1] cf. I Peter 1:3.

veloped by the premillenarians, is again burdened by the inconsistencies shown in Chapter VII, and therefore to be rejected.

Hence we conclude that Christ would be king of the promised land, the ancient inheritance of Israel, in such a way that Palestine is truly not excluded, but that eye hath not seen, and ear hath not heard and it hath not entered into the heart of man how great will be the inheritance of Abraham, the "heir of the world," Rom. 4:13.

"And, if ye are Christ's, then are ye Abraham's seed, heirs."[1] Then shall Christ reign over you throughout that inheritance, including "the world," yea, including that "salvation ready to be revealed in the last time."

3. *How Christ would be King over Israel.*

If Christ's kingship, then, over the land of promise, the inheritance of Abraham, is not to be limited to Canaan, but to be extended to the world, since Abraham becomes "heir of the world,"[2] what becomes of Christ's Messianic kingship over *Israel?*

Again, the spiritual interpretations of Israel, some of which were cited above,[3] point the way.

Jehovah will cause the tent of his covenant people to be enlarged.[4] *"The Holy One of Israel"*[5] *will enlarge his Israel, so as to "possess the nations."*[6] This gives rise to the kingship of the Messiah over his true and spiritual Israel, including Gentiles.

How inclusive will God's covenant people be, ac-

---
1) cf. Gal. 3:29.
2) cf. Rom. 4:13.
3) cf. Page 100.
4) cf. Isa. 54:2.
5) cf. Isa. 54:5.
6) cf. Isa. 54:3.

cording to this book of Isaiah? Will it be limited to Israel, after the flesh? Ah, no, far from it.

For this spiritual Israel shall "possess the nations." This involves the spiritual conquest of the nations.[1] It marks their inclusion into the covenant in its New Testament dispensation.[2]

For Isaiah says: *"Blessed be Egypt, my people, and Assyria, the work of my hands and Israel, mine inheritance."*[3]

Now the term "my people," here used for Egypt, is as much a description of Jehovah's covenant people, as is the term "mine inheritance," used here or Israel.[4] Hence the Gentiles receive as much a place in the covenant as does the Israel here mentioned.

And thus the Messiah would also reign over this enlarged covenant people, in such a way that he would become the mediator of the great blessing implied in these same words, "Blessed be Egypt, my people, and Assyria, the work of my hands, and Israel, mine inheritance."

Moreover the two Gentile nations, here mentioned, are intended to point to the believers of all the Gentiles, representatively, since Egypt and Assyria governed practically all the Gentile world of that time. Thus all Gentiles would be represented in the covenant.

Moreover, Isaiah also predicts the accession of the Gentiles, in general to Israel with the same universal intent elsewhere: "One shall say, I am

---
1) cf. The similar conquest in Amos 9:12, as spiritualized in Acts 15:17.
2) cf. Romans 11:16, and the ingrafted branches in verses 19 and 24.
3) cf. Isa. 19:25.
4) With "the work of my hands" of Isa. 19:25, compare 43:1, 44:21.

Jehovah's; and another shall call (himself) by the name of Jacob; and another shall subscribe with his hand unto Jehovah *and surname* (*himself*) *by the name of Israel.*"[1] Here, then, we have the Gentiles publicly professing their allegiance to Jehovah, and this attachment to his covenant people, Israel. For Gentiles will surname themselves by the name of Israel, and receive as much a right to the name of Israel as those Israelites that accept their ancient Jewish, ancestral, privileges in Jesus, the Messiah.

All this casts an interesting light upon the question, how the Messiah would be king over Israel.

There are, indeed, representations in the Old Testament, that Israel, under the Messiah's rule, would "possess the nations," as we saw above. But the New Testament interprets spiritually that possession. And what becomes of it is this, that the Gentiles seek the Lord and that they are admitted into the New Testament church,[2] which was at first largely Israelitish. Israel, therefore, has a temporal priority in the covenant.

But we also have the Old Testament representation that assigns no priority to Israel, — for instance, where Egypt and Assyria are mentioned ahead of Israel, among God's covenant people, as we saw above, and where Gentiles surname themselves by the name of Israel.

Here the Messiah would, evidently, rule over Israel in such a manner that Israel is put on a par with other nations; nay, rather that the saved of other nations are put on the same high and exalted plane

---
[1] cf. Isa. 44:5.
[2] cf. Acts 15:17 and Amos 9:12, and page 168.

with the true Israel, so far as their place in the covenant of the New Testament day is concerned.

Persons of other nations, therefore, do not here receive an inferior place in the commonwealth of Israel. On the contrary they are here in Isaiah as in the New Testament Scriptures, virtually made fellow-members in the covenant with Israel.[1]

Indeed, thus Paul also describes the exalted place of the Gentile Ephesians, as they are included by him with the saints of Israel.

For Paul makes it clear that the true Israel would include Ephesians, who were formerly *"Gentiles in the flesh, . . . alienated from the commonwealth of Israel,"*[2] *but are now "fellow-citizens with the saints,"*[3] . . . in the spiritual commonwealth, or kingdom,[4] of Israel.

Hence, in the prophesied reign of the Messiah, *that* Old Testament representation, in which Gentile believers are put on a par with Israelitish believers is evidently the representation adopted by the New Testament Scriptures. Hence, under the Messianic reign, the Gentile believers are, and will be, on the same exalted plane with the Israelitish saints, as their fellow-citizens, in the spiritual kingdom of Israel, and surnamed by the name of Israel.

Now should any Jew read these lines, let him not be offended at this. For he evidently does not need to leave Israel. But what he needs to do is to accept his ancestral privileges. We have long ago come over to Israel. We are even privileged to be fellow-

---
1) cf. Eph. 2:19.
2) cf. Eph. 2:12.
3) cf. Eph. 2:19.
4) Compare Col. 1:13, where the kingdom of the spiritual Israel also includes Gentiles.

citizens with the saints of Israel. Yea, we are even privileged to be fellow-citizens with the prophets, priests and kings of old, that were types of their exalted Messianic Redeemer, in the eternal[1] kingdom of God. For we serve under the eternally reigning Son of David, our Lord and Savior, Jesus Christ.

We are like unto the wild olive branches (in the figure of Paul), that were grafted into the tame olive tree. *And the olive tree is certainly Israel.*[2]

Again, the church is the New Testament bride of Christ.[3] But this bride is clearly identified with Israel in the Revelation of John. *For when the angel says: "Come hither, I will show thee the bride, the wife of the Lamb," John sees "the holy city, Jerusalem," whose gates are marked with the names of "the twelve tribes of the children of Israel."*[4]

Thus this true Israel of the Old and New Testament, including the Gentiles that have been added to the Church of Christ, will be represented by the holy city, Jerusalem. And this New Jerusalem will be ruled by our exalted Lord, Jesus Christ, in such a manner as to include the Gentiles that have been grafted into the good olive tree, Israel, and that have thus become fellow-citizens with the saints, though they had, in Old Testament times, been alienated from the commonwealth of Israel.[5]

It is clear, therefore, that though there is an Israel after the flesh, there is also an Israel after the spirit, of which Gentiles become fellow citizens, by being added to the church. Truly, there may be prophecies

---

1) cf. 2 Sam. 7:13-16; Isa. 9:7; Rev. 22:1.
2) cf. Romans 11:26, and the ingrafted branches in verses 19 and 24.
3) cf. John 3:29, 30; Mat. 9:15; Rev. 19:7, 8.
4) cf. Rev. 21:9-12.
5) cf. Eph. 2:12.

How Would Christ Become King of Zion? 155

that pertain specifically to the Israel, after the flesh, such as may concern their return again to the ancient holy land and their national conversion to Christ; but the prophecies as to the spiritual Israel concern the bride, the wife of the Lamb, the church of Christ, to which not only Ephesian Gentiles were added, but all Gentiles that become fellow-citizens with the saints of Israel, and that have surnamed themselves by the name of Israel. Hence it is this Israel, after the spirit, of which Christ would become king, according to the prophecies.

But how would Christ become king over this Israel, after the spirit?

As its king, the Messiah would have his path of humiliation and death, as well as his resurrection and exaltation.[1]

Thus only would the Messiah, the Servant of Jehovah,[2] the witness to the peoples,[3] represent the sure mercies of David,[4] as the eternal king on David's throne.[5]

To give an atoning basis to these sure mercies of David, he would pour out his soul unto death.[6] Yet God would not only make his soul an offering for sin. [7]But the Messianic Servant would prolong his days after death.[8] Yea, he would be exalted, and lifted up, and be very high.[9]

Kings would shut their mouths at him; for that which had not been told them should they see; and

---
1) cf. Isa. 52:13-53:12.
2) cf. Isa. 52:13.
3) cf. Isa. 55:4; compare the collective servant witnessing in Isa. 43:10.
4) cf. Isa. 55:3.
5) cf. 2 Sam. 7:13-16.
6) cf. Isa. 53:12.
7) cf. Isa. 53:10.
8) cf. Isa. 53:10.
9) cf. Isa. 52:13.

that which they had not heard, should they understand.[1]

Thus the Messianic king would experience great exaltation, as well as deep humiliation.

His humiliation would mark him as the humiliated Son of David, who would not come riding, like ancient monarchs and princes on horses or mules, but in the contrasted lowly fashion of the prophecy: "lowly, and riding upon an ass, even upon a colt, the foal of an ass."[2]

As the Passover Lamb was set apart unto death, several days before the Passover, so the humiliated Messiah would be set apart by the Scribes and Pharisees, unto his death, more than ever, at the Passover feast, on account of this royal, though lowly, entrance into Jerusalem.

For they feared an exaltation of this lowly "King of Israel."[3] But his exaltation was foretold to come, on account of the same atoning death of Calvary, an exaltation[4] as king of his entire spiritual Israel, — including its native and its engrafted branches.[5]

We have seen how Christ would be king of Jerusalem, in the light of Biblical generalizations and spiritualizations of Jerusalem or Zion. Similarly, we have observed how Christ would be king of the promised land, the inheritance of Abraham, in the light of its Biblical spiritualizations and generalizations. Again, we have noted how Christ would be king of Israel, in view of the Biblical enlargement

---
1) cf. Isa. 52:15.
2) cf. Zech. 9:9.
3) cf. John 12:13.
4) cf. Isa. 52:13-53:12.
5) cf. Rom. 11:19, 24, 26.

and spiritual interpretation of Israel, to include all believers.

Moreover, in the light of the foregoing spiritualizations of all the other vital elements of the theocracy, the corresponding applications to Christ's kingship might be continued. But they are self-evident.

Hence this is not necessary. Suffice it, therefore, to say, by way of summary, that the kingship of the prophesied Messiah would evidently come about amid the spiritual counterparts of the entire theocracy, as we find these counterparts in the church.

The elements of the typical, Old Testament kingdom, when spiritually interpreted, become the corresponding elements or phases of the antitypical, New Testament kingdom, namely the church.

This position is clearly seen to be Biblical, when we note that Christ identifies the kingdom and the church. For to Peter he says: "upon this rock I will build my *church* . . . I will give unto thee the keys of the kingdom of heaven," Mat. 16:18, 19. Here this kingdom and the church must be identical, — the typical Old Testament kingdom having made room for the antitypical, New Testament kingdom of heaven.

A similar identification of the New Testament kingdom with the church is involved in Paul's teaching that Gentiles, in being added to the church of God, are brought over "into the kingdom of the Son of his love," Col. 1:13.

Similarly, the identification of the church, as the bride of Christ, with the kingdom of Israel, having the New Jerusalem as its capital, is involved in Revelation 21:9-12.

All this evidence shows very clearly that Christ would become king of this New Jerusalem, by becoming the king of the church.

And so, if the New Testament kingdom is thus identified with the church, it is clear that we may, likewise, consider the Old Testament typical kingdom to have found its New Testament counterpart in the church and its Messianic king in the king and head of the *kingdom* of heaven," Mat. 16:18, 19, the church of our Lord and Savior, Jesus Christ.

His we are and Him we serve, our Blessed Redeemer, the Lord of Glory. Praise be to God for his unspeakable mercy, in having given us the privilege that we, too, might be brought over into "the kingdom of the Son of his love," Col. 1:13.

CHAPTER IX

HOW DID CHRIST BECOME KING OF JERUSALEM?

Christ's predicted kingship over Jerusalem, the Zion of God, represents the end and purpose, in many of the prophecies concerning the future of the typical kingdom. Can the prophecies of this Messianic kingship over Zion be interpreted in the light of any recorded fulfillments?

Does any recorded fulfillment speak of *the throne of David,* and if so, how? Says Peter on Pentecost: "Brethren, I may say unto you freely of the patriarch *David,* that he both died and was buried, and his tomb is with us unto this day. Being therefore a prophet, and knowing that God had sworn with an oath to him, that of the fruit of his loins he would set one *upon his throne;* he foreseeing this spake of the resurrection of the Christ, that neither was he left unto Hades, nor did his flesh see corruption. This Jesus did God raise up, whereof we all are witnesses. Being therefore by the right hand of God *exalted,* and having received of the Father the promise of the Holy Spirit, he hath poured forth this, which ye see and hear. For David ascended not into the heavens; but he saith himself,

> The Lord said unto my Lord, *Sit thou on my right hand,*
> Till I make thine enemies the footstool of thy feet.

Let all the house of Israel therefore know assuredly, that *God hath made him both Lord and Christ,* this Jesus whom ye crucified." Acts 2:29-36.

Now does it not seem as if Christ's sitting on the throne of David is here curiously identified with his sitting at the right hand of the Father, to govern his spiritual Zion, the Church?

But so sweeping a conclusion may well be tested, by comparing other New Testament fulfillments, in their interrelations. Such comparison is especially necessary, for so important a fulfillment, as this present one. It is like the top of a great pyramid.

This is the royal climax of the fulfillments, which we are now to consider. The New Testament cites many fulfillments of prophecy. These give us the opportunity to test our conclusion that Christ's kingship is spiritual over his spiritual Zion. To this position all the evidence of the previous chapter leads directly or indirectly, in spiritualizing all the elements of this kingdom, including Jerusalem, Zion, Israel, and the inheritance promised to Abraham.

The many recorded New Testament fulfillments show us how Christ actually became the spiritual king of his priestly kingdom, the church. They thus gloriously vindicate our interpretation of the eschatology of the theocracy, — the future of the kingdom, I Peter 2:9, as "a royal priesthood, a holy nation," identified with the church, 2:10.

Let us therefore now consider the *Resultant Construction of the future of the O. T. Kingdom* as based on these principles, and more particularly as clarified and reinforced by fulfillments vouched for in the New Testament itself.

How then would evidently the Primary Author, the Holy Spirit, have one view the future of the O. T. kingdom? In other words, to what results do the hermeneutical or interpretive principles, latent in the Old Testament, and evident in the New, lead in the interpretation of the Old Testament materials in question? The final result to which the Holy Spirit as the Primary Author of Scripture would evidently have us come with respect to the future of the O. T. kingdom must surely not be sought in a denial of the latent and evident spiritualization that the Holy Spirit himself furnishes us. Hence it cannot be found in an earthly millennium, as such.

But it must be sought after the manner, indicated by the Holy Spirit, in the spiritualizations cited in the previous chapter. And then it is found in the kingdom of grace of the New Testament era, together with its glorious consummation in the kingdom of glory. For the kingdom of glory (Rev. 22:1) is the final, eternal (Isa. 9:6) state of the kingdom of grace. Meanwhile, the kingdom of grace is evidently identified with the church, in Mat. 16:18, 19, by our Lord, Jesus Christ, himself, and by Paul in Col. 1:13.

Now this construction is clarified and reinforced also especially when we note the individual prophecies, concerning the future of the O. T. kingdom that the New Testament actually recognizes to have been fulfilled in the N. T. period.

Moreover, when we note the fulfillments of these definite prophecies we can, from them, construe the future of this kingdom more in detail, upon the unimpeachable basis of the direct interpretation of this eschatology by the Primary Author, the Holy Spirit, himself.

These specially mentioned fulfillments relate to prophecies concerning each of the theocratic offices, prophet, priest, and king.

We shall take up these offices in this order, since Christ's royal task is illuminated by his prophetic message and the reward of his priestly work, forming the acme and climax.

For Christ became the great, eternal king of his spiritual Jerusalem, the church, on the basis of his mediatorial, priestly work, and as interpreted by his prophetic office. What then is recognized as fulfilled?

A. — THE PROPHETIC OFFICE AND THE N. T. FULFILLMENT OF THE GREAT MOSAIC PROPHECY RELATING TO IT

There are several places in the N. T. that record the fulfillment of this prophecy.

1. Moses' prophecy, Deut. 18:15, fulfilled in John 5:46. Not only does Moses then foretell a prophet like unto himself, but Christ indicates the fulfillment of this prophecy to the Jews, — "For if ye believed Moses, ye would believe me; for he wrote of me," John 5:46. Now the only direct Messianic prophecy which Moses gave, in his own name, is that of Deut. 18:15, just referred to.

2. Deut. 18:15 had in view in John 1:45. It was, furthermore, no doubt chiefly this passage of the Pentateuch that Philip had in view, when he said to Nathanael, "We have found him of whom Moses in the law, and prophets wrote, Jesus of

Nazareth . . . " (Cf. also John 6:14; 4:45; Luke 11:50, 51; 24:19.)

3. Again Deut. 18:15 referred to in Acts 3:22; 7:37. In Acts 3:22 and 7:37, there are, moreover, references of Peter and Stephen to the prophet foretold of Moses, with the implications that Christ had fulfilled this prophecy. The great eschatological prophet, of whom all the theocratic prophets were typical, is, therefore, regarded by the New Testament, as having come in Christ, in fulfillment of the prophecy. Of course, Christ's prophetic work goes on, but there is no reason to hold that it will again have a special manifestation, in a physical return of his, during an earthly millennium, while sin continues, before his penetrating, righteous eyes. For his denunciations of sin would bring about either another Calvary or a Judgment Day, long before the end of the millennium.

In other words, Christ's prophetic work, when in the flesh he taught on earth amid sin, involved a humiliation that is ended. He is now in heaven the great prophet of his spiritual Zion, the church. There, as prophet, he still illumines, through the preaching of the Word, not only his present kingship over his spiritual Zion, the church, but also his final kingship over this Zion, in glory.

Moreover, his disciples, continuing his prophetic teaching, show, in the following evidence from the New Testament, what Christ really teaches concerning the manner of fulfillment of the prophecies of his priestly sacrifice, the foundation laid for his royal tasks.

Let us see next, then, how these fulfillments concerning his priestly work are thus interpreted, in the New Testament.

B. — THE PRIESTLY OFFICE IN O. T. PROPHECIES THAT HAVE EXPLICIT N. T. FULFILLMENTS OR ALLUSIONS

There are also recognized fulfillments of certain prophecies dealing with the eschatological priest or priest-king, and with the eschatology of the sacrifical system of the theocracy.

1. Zech. 3:8; Compare Heb. 8:3. Now since the O. T. High Priest was typical, and the high priest Joshua and his fellow-priests were even called typical men, Zech. 3:8, the Epistle to the Hebrews shows Christ to be the antitypical High Priest, — "For every high priest is appointed to offer both gifts and sacrifices; wherefore it is necessary that this (high priest) also have somewhat to offer." (Hebrews 8:3).

2. Isa. 42:1-4; Compare Mat. 12:7-21. The humiliated priest-king, the Servant of Jehovah, is not only the subject of Isaiah's prophecy, but the fulfillment of the Servant prophecies is expressly identified with the earthly life and passion of Christ. For Matthew (12:7-21) sees in Jesus' healing the sick a fulfillment of the Servant prophecy of Isa. 42:1-4.

3. Isa. 53:7; Compare Acts 8:32-35. And when the Ethiopian reading Isa. 53 asked Philip, "I pray thee, of whom speaketh the prophet this?", Philip

"beginning from this Scripture, preached unto him Jesus." (Acts 8:32-35.)

4. Ps. 110:5, Compare Hebrews 5:6, 10, 6:20; 7:15. Meanwhile, the priestly Messianic reference of Psalm 110, in verse 4, —

> "Thou art a priest forever
> After the order of Melchizedek,"

is also quoted, as is clear from Hebrews 5:6, 10; cf. 6:20; 7:17. Nor is this part of the psalm interpreted as waiting until a millennium, for itsfillment, but as reaching its fulfillment in Christ's present priestly work, and emphatically without the continuance or resumption of bloody sacrifices, Hebrews 10:10.

5. Ezekiel 47:1-10; Compare John 4:10; Rev. 22:1; Mat. 4:19. Again, these prophecies and their fulfillments form such an organic unity that corresponding fulfillments of kindred priestly prophecies would seem to be implied. Compare the living waters of the temple-river of Ezek. 47:1 with the living waters of John 4:10 and Rev. 22:1. — Ezek. 47:10; Compare Mat. 4:19.

In chapters 40-48, some elements of Ezekiel's vision evidently suggest Old Testament reforms, such as the reorganization of the priesthood, limiting to the sons of Zadok the administration of the cultus, including sin- and trespass-offerings. All this had its meaning for the nearer perspective, the more immediate future of the Old Testament theocratic regime, while atoning sin-offerings would never fit in any millennium, after Christ's atonement.

But there are other parts of Ezekiel 40-48 that contain references applying to the more distant perspective of the New Testament dispensation. For the mention of living waters, by Christ, to the Samaritan Woman at Jacob's Well, and the references to fishers of men suggest an initial fulfillment of this vision in the New Testament dispensation.

Meanwhile, the unsullied, perfectly pure waters, clear as crystal, in the vision of the waters of life, in the last chapter of Revelation, suggest the final and perfect fulfillment of Ezekiel's vision, in the New Jerusalem, after the final Judgment Day.

C. — THE ROYAL OFFICE IN O. T. PROPHECIES HAVING EXPLICIT N. T. FULFILLMENTS OR ALLUSIONS

The future Davidic king would, furthermore, according to the principles of interpretation derived, not be a king of this world, (kosmos not 'aioon, age) in an earthly millennium, but a spiritual king, in the spiritual kingdom of the New Testament era, as well as when he comes to judge "all these that are in the graves," (John 5:27-29), both the saved and the lost, yea both the quick and the dead, and to usher in the final state.

Now, there are also a number of individual, Messianic, *royal* prophecies that the New Testament regards as having been fulfilled during Christ's earthly sojourn, and with none of these recognized fulfillments is there the suggestion that these prophecies must once more be fulfilled, in a more glorious fashion, during an earthly millennium.

1. Micah 5:1; Compare Mat. 2:6. We have, then first of all, the prophecy of the Messiah's rise from Bethlehem. Not only does Micah foretell this origin of the Messiah, as the Son of David. But the knowledge of this prophecy, on the part of the chief priests and the scribes enables Herod to direct the Wise Men, on their journey, — according to Mat. 2:6, where Micah's prophecy is expressly quoted.

Now, it is argued that the literal fulfillment of this prophecy is an indication that the other Messianic prophecies must also be fulfilled literally.

But many Messianic prophecies involve the spiritualizations evidenced above, in Chapter VIII. And then, of course, we are permitted to employ the spiritual interpretations thus evidenced, in interpreting these Messianic prophecies.

However, we do not find that Bethlehem is spiritualized expressly by the Scriptures, to signify anything else than the original town of Bethlehem, as the home of David. As such, it emphasizes Christ's rise from this lowly home of King David.

Thus it accentuates the idea of Christ's lowliness, which fits in entirely with the organic unity of ideas expressed by Christ's humiliation. Moreover, it represents the Messiah's descent from King David, to fulfill the promises involved in the sure mercies of David (2 Sam. 7:13; Isa. 55:3).

2. Amos 9:11, 12; Compare Acts 15:16-18. Not only would the Davidic dynasty be restored and rule through war over its ancient enemy Edom, according to Amos 9. But in Acts 15:18, all this is applied by James to the situation in hand. For here Christ's exalted reign from heaven represents the glorious restoration of the dynasty, the remnant of Edom becomes the residue of men, the military possession of Edom makes room for the voluntary seeking of the Gentiles after the Lord, with the absence of the physical warfare, suggested by the imagery of Amos.

Nor can James have reference to a future millennium, when he quotes the words, "After these things will I return." For he has just said, "And to this agree the words of the prophets," — his purpose is therefore to enforce what Simon Peter had just contended, concerning the extension of the "word of the gospel" (V. 7.) unto the Gentiles. His purpose is, therefore, contemporaneous and not millennial.

Of course, it can here be shown that this spiritualization had its antecedents in the Septuagint, with textual critical matters bearing upon the situation. But in the New Testament, we have here the official stamp of approval placed upon the principle of spiritualization by the Primary Author himself. Instead of Edom, as well as the other nations, going back to their ancient habitats, to be ruled by Israel, the rule over the Gentile nations proceeds from the heavenly exalted Christ, through "the word of the gospel," as proclaimed by the great spiritual kingdom under his sway, and through all the agencies ordained by him who has given the keys of the kingdom to the officers of the church, that is built upon the confession of Peter.

When Isaiah 9 tells us that the people that dwelt in darkness have seen a great light, there is an implied contrast with a previous state of "contempt," due to the ravages of war. For "in the former time he brought into contempt the land of Zebulun and Naphtali; but in the latter time hath he made it glorious ... " Again Isaiah introduces military language into the succeeding context, — "For the yoke of his burden, and the staff of his shoulder, the rod of his oppressor thou hast broken as in the day of Midian."

Hence the imagery of the prophecy suggests physical, miliary conquests to offset the previous military degredation of the land, conquests that would accompany the rise of the supernatural Prince of Peace to the throne of David. But though the gospels do show us that Christ is supernatural and mighty God, yet the great Son of David that appears in the land of Zebulun and Naphtali makes all his conquests without either the military means or the throne of David suggested by Isaiah's prophecy.

Nevertheless, Mat. 4:13 quotes, as "fulfilled," the prophecy that "to them that sat in the region and shadow of death, to them did light spring up." This lets us see what was in the mind of the Primary Author, the Holy Spirit, when he gave the prophecy to Isaiah. It involved a spiritual eschatological outlook, a spiritual, eschatological conquest, though it might suggest military conquest and a physical throne to the reader.

We can see the essence of the prophecy, in the form, because of its New Testament fulfillment, and divest it of its imagery; the Old Testament saints received the essence of the prophecy, without, as a rule, being able to divest it of the imagery in which it was couched. But, for the Primary Author, the Spirit of God, the essence of the prophecy corresponds perfectly to its fulfillment. Of course, the fulfillment includes the conquest of the final Judgment Day.

3. Zech. 9:9; Compare Mat. 21:4, 5. Not only does Zechariah 9:9 look forward to the royal rule of the Son of David, though begun in lowliness,

> "Rejoice greatly, O daughter of Zion, . . .
> Behold thy king cometh unto thee."

But Matthew 21:4, 5 tells us, at the Triumphal Entry of Christ, "Now this is come to pass," evidently showing no hesitation in considering Christ king, on that occasion; for he is called "thy king," without suggesting, in any way a kingship over a millennial kingdom.

4. Ps. 110:1; Compare Acts 2:34-36. However, also the exalted priest-king of Ps. 110 is identified with Christ, without the slightest intimation that there is still a more literal fulfillment of this prophetic psalm to be expected in an earthly millennium, on an earthly throne of David.

Not only do we then have the royal Messiah foretold in Ps. 110:1,

> "Sit thou at my right hand,
> Until I make thine enemies thy footstool."

But this prophecy receives a spiritual interpretation in Acts 2:34-36, where it is expressly stated that "David ascended not into the heavens," but that God hath made this Jesus, whom the Jews had crucified, "both Lord and Christ." The same spiritual interpretation is implied in the following passages, Acts 5:31; Eph. 1:20, 22; Col. 3:1; Heb. 1:3; 8:1; 10:12.

5. Ps. 110:1; Compare I Cor. 15:25. Furthermore, this verse, Ps. 110:1, is interpreted in connection with Christ's Second Coming in I Cor. 15:25, "For he must reign till he hath put all enemies under his feet." But in this context again, there is absolutely no suggestion of an earthly millennium, while the previous verse even militates against it, — "Then cometh the end when he shall deliver up the kingdom to God, even the Father." For the millenarians have the expectation, — "Then cometh the end of this age, when he shall inaugurate the millennial kingdom on earth." But Paul does not imply this when he applies this passage to the future.

There would seem to be no ground for holding any other position than that the eschatological priest-king of Ps. 110:1 must be interpreted, in the light of the New Testament, as even now sharing in the royal honor foretold, and about to share still more in that honor, when the last enemy, death, shall be abolished. For there is no New Testament quotation or interpretation of this passage that requires its application to an earthly, millennial reign.

6. Dan. 7:13, 14; Compare Mat. 26:64. Not only does the Son of Man appear in Dan. 7, as a royal figure, to whom is given 'dominion and glory and a kingdom," whose "dominion is an everlasting dominion, which shall not pass away, and his Kingdom that which shall not be destroyed." But before the highest tribunal of the theocratic nation, which was soon to lose this official position among the nations, Jesus testifies, "Henceforth ye shall see the Son of Man sitting at the right hand of Power, . . . " Mat. 26:64. His spiritual kingdom, "not of this world" would thus be ruled.

The organic unity of these prophecies and their fulfillment implies also a coresponding fulfillment of kindred royal prophecies, like that of Gen. 49:10.

On the basis of the expressly recognized fulfillments and interpretations, of certain Messianic royal prophecies, we may say that the others would also be fulfilled in the same predominantly spiritual way, for they form an organic, spiritual unity. For instance, in the Shiloh prophecy, the sceptre and the ruler's staff must certainly be understood as spiritually as the military conquest and the throne of David, in Isa. 9.

All this shows us how Christ did become King of his spiritual Jerusalem, the church, the Zion of God.[1]

---

[1] cf. St. Augustine's City of God.

CHAPTER X

THE BIBLICAL SCOPE OF SPIRITUALLY INTERPRETED PROPHECY AND OF LITERAL FULFILLMENTS

One must approach this subject with great care. For it represents the conclusions toward which all the previous investigations lead. Meanwhile very little has been written on this topic with the express purpose of giving evidence not only for spiritual interpretations but also for literal fulfillments.

For most treatments are specially concerned to establish either kind of interpretation for well nigh all prophecies, either the so-called spiritual or the literal, — supported with examples.

Now the peculiar phenomenon is that examples can be cited for both literal fulfillments and spiritual And so the question arises, which prophecies must be interpreted literally and which permit of spiritual interpretation?

A survey of literally fulfilled predictions was given at the beginning of Chapter III. These represent a large sphere and realm of literally interpreted prophecies, and their number could be increased, especially from the life of Christ.

But if the scope of spiritualization can be indicated in Scripture, and if the organic unity can be pointed out that unites prophetic elements to be spiritualized, then this suggests, at least in broad outline, the dividing line between predictions to be interpreted literally, and prophecies to be understood spiritually.

What then is the scope of spiritualization?

A. — SURVEY OF THE SCOPE OF SPIRITUALIZATION IN SCRIPTURE, INVOLVING THE ORGANIC UNITY OF THE TYPICAL KINGDOM, AS THIS KINGDOM FINDS ITS FULFILLMENT IN THE CHURCH

Evidence is naturally desired on such a question.[1] Now the evidence has been cited for the spiritual interpretation of all the vital phases of the Old Testament kingdom, as they appear in prophecy. This evidence shows that the Scriptures incipiently spiritualize, in the Old Testament, and more fully spiritualize in the New Testament the following elements or phases of the theocracy:

1. Zion or Jerusalem, its capital; (See pages 88 and 144).
2. The promised land, the inheritance of the saints; (See pages 91 and 147).
3. The kingdom; (See pages 94, 118, 143, 166, 174, 176).
4. The seed of Abraham; (See page 97).
5. The covenant people, as the bride of the Lord; (See page 98).
6. Israel; (See pages 100 and 150).
7. Israel's enemies, as typified in the Edomites; (See pages 108 and 168).

VIII, represents a paper read before the Chicago Society of Biblical Research, October 21, 1933.
1) Chapter X, together with the Biblical evidence given in Chapter

8. The physical conquest of the enemies of the kingdom, as spiritualized into their spiritual conquest and voluntary obedience; (See pages 111-112).
9. The temple and the sacrifices; (Page 113).
10. Priestly, royal and prophetic types; (Page 116).
11. The old covenant; (See page 121).
12. Its sacraments; (See pages 134 and 135).

That the spiritual interpretation of the above, typical items directs one's attention to their counterparts in the church of Jesus Christ has been demonstrated above. (Cf. Chapter VIII).

But how must one arrive at a conclusion as to which prophecies were intended literally and which spiritually? Has not the Spirit given us some light, through these spiritualizations?

B. — HOW APPLY THE SCRIPTURAL GUIDANCE THUS GIVEN, TO TEACH US WHETHER A PROPHECY WAS EVIDENTLY INTENDED LITERALLY, OR WHETHER IT INVOLVED THE SPIRITUAL INTERPRETATION OF ONE OR MORE ITEMS

Now, in asking whether a prophecy was intended to be understood literally or spiritually, there are certain more specific questions that would seem to lead to the meaning of the Spirit.

1. *The First Question.*

Hence the first question is with respect to any item: *Does the Scripture spiritualize this item?* If evidence has not been adduced for the spiritualization of this item, *can that evidence be produced?* For instance, the question may be raised, may one interpret in a spiritual way, the promised land, or Zion, or Israel? Certainly it is then in order to show that the Scriptures actually do interpret spiritually these cardinal items.

It must be admitted that the accumulation of the evidence in question directs the attention to its organic unity.

For we may conclude that all this leads us to observe the Biblical scope of the spiritual interpretation of prophecy. For the entire body of concepts spiritualized by the Scriptures combines to represent the vital and permanent elements of the Old Testament Kingdom that reappear in spiritualized form in the spiritual, New Testament kingdom, namely the church.

2. *The Second Question.*

This leads to a second question with respect to any item. It points to the manner of testing to see whether a given prophecy is to be interpreted literally or whether the spiritual interpretations will satisfy its requirements.

For the great question now is: *Does the prophecy logically allign itself to the church? Does it logically fit into the organic unity, represented by the church? More specifically, does a prophecy, with reference to the future of the typical kingdom fit in organically with the future of the church?*

If so, we have no right to say that it requires more than a spiritual fulfillment in the church. The demands and requirements of the prophecy will have been met by such a spiritual fulfillment.

We, as mere creatures, have therefore, absolutely no right to say that such a prophecy still requires a literal fulfillment.

Of course, the sovereign Lord is always free to give the prophecy a more literal fulfillment than the prophecy itself requires. But we, on our part, have no right to attempt to hold the Lord to literal fulfillments in such cases, in view of the many spiritualizations in God's Word and particularly in the light of the spiritual fulfillments especially recognized as such in the New Testament.

Now the Biblical passages, treated in Chapter VIII, showing how Christ would become king of Zion, of the promised land and of Israel, all fit into the organic unity represented by the church, and have accordingly been so applied.

Moreover, from the way in which prophecies have been fulfilled in Christ Jesus, we have also observed the Biblical scope of spiritually interpreted prophecies.

Thus we have seen that the scope of these spiritually interpreted prophecies is clearly such that the typical Old Testament kingdom makes room for the antitypical New Testament kingdom, identified by Christ with his church.

Besides, we have observed especially that no indication is given, by the New Testament Scriptures, that a more literal fulfillment, in an earthly kingdom, is a part of the plan of God.

Hence we may conclude that it becomes entirely unfair, to the Scriptures, to attempt to hold them to the view of such a more literal fulfillment in the future. For the accomplished New Testament fulfillments, as especially recognized in Scripture, do not raise this expectation.

Hence these fulfillments serve as a vindication of that which has been seen in the preceding spiritualizations.

Now in the above two questions or tests, we thus have a guide, in the interpretation of other passages that refer to various elements or phases of the Old Testament typical kingdom and to its antitheocratic enemies.

3. *Application to Prophecies and to other Biblical Passages.*

Now how must one interpret such a reference to Zion or Jerusalem, as the following?

"Pray for the peace of Jerusalem,
They shall prosper that love thee."—Psalm 122:6.

Of course, the allusion includes originally ancient Jerusalem, as the rest of the psalm indicates. But is the reference limited to that? Clearly Jerusalem has been generalized and spiritualized in Scripture. Moreover, the present verse fits logically with those texts that refer to Jerusalem in such a manner that the church is clearly involved.

It is therefore evidently in the light of those spiritualizing texts that one should pray for the peace of Jerusalem today, and therefore pray for the church.

But there are other references to Zion or Jerusalem that cannot be thus applied. Such passages, not fitting into the organic unity represented by the church, must therefore not be spiritually but literally interpreted.

The Biblical Scope of Spiritualization

For instance: "Zion shall be plowed as a field," Micah 3:12. It can hardly be said that the church will be plowed as a field! This prophecy must evidently be understood literally and was in fact literally fulfilled, as we have seen.[1]

Similarly, the Messiah would come into Jerusalem, "riding upon an ass, even upon a colt, the foal of an ass," Zech. 9:9. It would become incongruous to say that the Messiah would ride into the church in that fashion. This prophecy must, therefore, also be understood literally, and was in fact so fulfilled,[2] though it also emphasizes humility.

Again, there are literal prophecies concerning Samaria, the capital city of the northern kingdom of Israel, — in Micah 1:6: "Therefore I will make Samaria as a heap of the field, and as places for planting vineyards; and I will pour down the stones thereof into the valley and I will uncover the foundations thereof."[3]

This, too, does not fit organically into the complex of ideas and realities represented by the church, and must, therefore, be understood literally. In fact, all these prophecies were fulfilled literally, as we were privileged to see, in Palestine, in 1931.

The stones of Old Tyre would be cast into the sea, according to Ezekiel 26:12: "They shall lay thy stones and thy timber and thy dust in the midst of the waters." Everyone realizes that this prophecy does not apply to the complex realities associated with the church, but that it must be understood lit-

---
1) cf. Chapter I, page 20.
2) cf. John 12:13.
3) cf. Chapter I, page 19.

erally, as it was indeed fulfilled.[1] It cannot even be applied to the antitheocratic world as such, in a more general and typical way.

In the same way, numerous other prophecies referring to Palestine and other Bible lands, can be matched with literal fulfillments. A survey of these prophecies was given at the opening of Chapter III. These represent a fairly complete list of the predictions concerning Bible lands that have been fulfilled literally, though others could be added whose interpretation is somewhat problematical.[2]

These prophecies show, in a measure, the scope of literally fulfilled prophecies. For none of these prophecies fit in organically with the future of the church. They therefore might be expected to be fulfilled literally, as they have been, in fact. To expect them to be fulfilled, specifically, once more, in the enemies of the New Testament church is without sufficient Scriptural basis.

Meanwhile, we may, indeed, attempt to learn from the manner in which the Lord may be bringing about literal fulfillments in our day and age.

Palestine, today, represents a tremendous contrast of desolate places and of reclaimed beauty spots that are wonderful.

Do we not have, then, today, in a measure at least, the fulfillment of the prophecies that the once Holy Land would be waste,[3] but that the desert would also again blossom as a rose?[4]

---

1) cf. Chapter I, page 14.
2) cf. "The Wonders of Prophecy," by John Urquhart; "De Stipte en Letterlijke Vervulling der Bybelsche Profetien," by A. Keith; and "Fulfilled Prophecies That Prove the Bible," by G. T. B. Davis.
3) cf. Lev. 26:30-33; Deut. 29:22; Isa. 8:11, 12; Ezek. 36:33-35.
4) cf. Ezek. 36:33-38; Jer. 49:6.

The Biblical Scope of Spiritualization

The top of Mount Carmel is now well nigh treeless, though it has many beautiful trees on its slopes, and on the desert plains below, partly reclaimed. Do we not here have the fulfillment of Amos' words:

"The pastures of the shepherds shall mourn
And the top of Carmel shall wither."—Amos 1:2.

Many Jewish colonies today dot the land of Palestine in villages of their own, on land in part reclaimed from desert desolation. Are we not warranted in seeing prophecies fulfilled in this partial return of the Jews? Think of Ezekiel 38:8:

"After many days thou shalt be visited: in the latter days thou shalt come into the land that is brought back (or restored) from the sword, that is gathered out of many peoples, upon the mountains of Israel, which have been a continual waste; but it is brought forth out of thy peoples, and they shall dwell securely, all of them."

Though the enemy Gog is addressed here, something is also implied as to Israel's return to their ancient home, the once holy land. For it will be a land restored from the sword. Nay more, it will be inhabited by a people gathered out of many peoples, upon the mountains of Israel, which have been a continual waste. That people shall be brought forth out of all peoples. And they shall dwell securely all of them, apparently on the ancient mountains of Israel.

Now the latter days, involving Gog, are applied, in the book of Revelation,[1] to a Gog, toward the end

---
1) cf. Rev. 20:8.

of time. The present prophecy of Ezekiel is in the Revelation of John, applied to the future, at least in part, and probably still awaits fulfillment.

But the restoration of Israel to their old home is not explicitly thus applied to the future, in the Book of Revelation.

Yet Ezekiel's prophecy may involve two horizons. The one then would lie in our future, on which appears the Gog of Revelation. The other horizon would then involve the post-exilic return to Palestine under Joshua, Zerubbabel, Ezra and Nehemiah.

In this latter sense the return to Palestine to which Ezekiel here may refer is past, though in the former sense the prophecy would have a repeated fulfillment, if it must be so interpreted.

4. *The Jewish Return to Palestine as a Literal Fulfillment?*

Hence the question arises, What is the scope of Israel's present return to Palestine? To anyone who has traveled through Palestine and noted the number of Jewish colonies, and Jewish efforts to make the land blossom as a rose, as at Tel Abib, and elsewhere, the Jewish return to Palestine would seem to be sufficient to consider the prophecy of Ezekiel in this respect incipiently fulfilled, if it is so intended.

The history of Zionism points to the same general conclusion.

But are the historical developments in Palestine significant enough to be worthy of consideration, in connection with prophecies that may be concerned?

If Judah sang psalms of joy and gratitude at its return from exile, seeing the fulfillment of prophecies in this return, what shall we say as to the ten tribes of the northern kingdom of Israel, from which but a mere representation returned? Did the ten tribes defeat the prophecies of the return from exile? This can scarcely be held. The prophecies were fulfilled unto those that complied with their requirements. The same principle may be applied today, to the solution of our problem.

If then the ten tribes remained, all but a few individuals, in the land of exile, so that but a mere representation of these tribes returned, what shall we say concerning the prosperous Jews in New York, Chicago, and elsewhere, that manifest no intention of living in Palestine, at a very early date? Do they defeat the alleged fulfillment of adduced prophecies? Not if many other Jews do go to the once holy land.

If the Jews that returned to Palestine after the exile, in the days of Joshua, Zerubbabel, Ezra and Nehemiah, numbered approximately 50,000, what shall we say concerning the hundred thousand Jews in Palestine, when the world war began, a number that has increased remarkably ever since? These Jews in Palestine today may also be considered as a fulfillment of the predictions, when these prophecies are understood accordingly.

If the Jews after the exile for a long time had no independent government, but were under Persia, what shall we say of a statement like the following? This was made in 1917 by Lord Balfour, British Minister of Foreign Affairs, in a letter to Lord Rothschild: "The government views with favor the establishment of Palestine as a national home for the Jewish people and will use its best endeavors to facilitate the achievement of this object." Does not this suggest that the adduced prophecies may be fulfilled in even a more glorious fashion, than were the prophecies touching Israel's return from exile?

If, after Israel had taken Canaan, under Moses' successor, Joshua, the Canaanite was still in the land, and if when the exiles from Babylonia had occupied Palestine, various kinds of Canaanites were again in the land, what shall we say as to the Arabic-speaking natives still in Palestine today? Can they be regarded as completely nullifying the adduced prophecies? Certainly the prophecies, so understood, are being fulfilled sufficiently.

If the returned exiles, under Joshua and Zerubbabel, Ezra and Nehemiah had to build, with their swords at hand, for fear of the natives, what shall we say of the comparatively peaceful possession by the Jews of many beautiful places (upwards of 300,000 acres of land in Palestine valued at $50,000,000, circa 1931)? This, too, suggests a broad fulfillment of the prophecies, if so intended.

If, after the exile, Judah first settled around Jerusalem and in the south, in the ancient territory of Judah, only gradually peopling the north, what shall we say concerning the present Jewish colonies that have attained to great beauty near Jaffa, that occupy approximately a quarter of Jerusalem and that are scattered along the beautiful Jordan and on those reclaimed wastes of the Plain of Esdraelon where once reigned desolation but where the land again begins to blossom as the rose? Once more, it would

The Biblical Scope of Spiritualization

seem that the prophecies are surely being fulfilled, if they must be so understood.

If the returning exiles had such a forlorn existence in Palestine as to cause the face of Nehemiah to mourn before his king,[1] what shall we say concerning the prosperity of the Jewish places near Jaffa, and concerning the estimated value of agricultural products grown by various Jewish colonies in Palestine (each year, as approximately $8,750,000, now) and of the beauty of the Jewish places along the Jordan? Certainly again it would seem that the fulfillments of today are more advanced than were the fulfillments in the days of Nehemiah.

If the returned exiles had to be content with buying or growing the ordinary Palestinian foods,[2] what shall we say concerning the luxury represented by the cultivation and exportation of oranges, especially from the region of the Jewish colonies near Jaffa (when it is reported that the Palestine orange crop of 1929 amounted to 4,000,000 boxes, each weighing 70 pounds), wonderful oranges that find a ready market in Europe? Must we still insist on a greater fulfillment? We should be satisfied even if we could not cite such literal fulfillments to the prophecies that speak of the desert blossoming as the rose.

If the returned exiles had to be reproached by Ezra for marrying foreign wives,[3] what shall we say as to the marked isolation in this respect of the Jewish people today, especially in Palestine? Does not this people still live alone in a large measure?[4]

---
1) cf. Neh. 2:2.
2) cf. Neh. 13:15.
3) cf. Ezra 10:10.
4) cf. Num. 23:9.

If the returning exiles had to contend with the surrounding Ammonites, Ashdodites, Canaanites and Arabians,[1] what shall we say of the opinion, found among archaeologists,[2] that the lowest social class, today, in Palestine and the surrounding countries, includes descendants of the ancient, native Canaanites, and their neighbors? Moreover, this poverty-stricken, native population is subjected or combated by the upper ruling class, whether Turks, or British, and by the powerful Jews, — like the house of the Rothschilds, the great British banking house, now influential in Palestine. Hence, if Israel's presence, in Palestine, should presuppose their dominating influence over their ancient enemies, these enemies may be represented among the down-trodden natives today, of Palestine and its environs; and prophecy, thus understood, might still be regarded as fulfilled.

If the walls of Jerusalem were still down, in the time of Nehemiah, what shall we say of the beautiful Palestinian architectural structures of the Jews today such as the Jewish University near Jerusalem, the Tel Abib buildings and those near the Jordan?

If our Lord Jesus Christ prophesied the destruction of the temple, so that not one stone would be left upon the other and that prophecy was literally fulfilled and the Jews even with the help of the Emperor Julian the Apostate were not able to rebuild the temple, why should we look for the Jews to build the temple again in modern times? It is not to be expected.

---

1) cf. Neh. 4:7.
2) cf. M. G. Kyle's "Excavating Kirjath-Sepher's Ten Cities," page 193.

THE BIBLICAL SCOPE OF SPIRITUALIZATION   187

If the returning Jews became very self-righteous in the time of Malachi, what shall we say as to the gathering of Jews from all over the world that met at Jerusalem recently and voted that they as a people had made a grievous error in condemning Jesus of Nazareth to death, an error that must be set right or the blood of Jesus would continue to come upon them and their children?

If there is foretold a hardening of the people "until the fulness of the Gentiles shall come in"[1] what else could we expect than the large measure of unbelief that there has been among the Jews. Yet the hardening is not general, according to Romans 11, nor everlasting, in the view of many commentators. Even now, there are many converted Jews, — all over the world.

If there was a remnant of the Jews according to the election of grace "at the present time"[2] as well as their hardening "unto this very day," shall we not rejoice at the proportions of that saved remnant of Israel?

"The Presbyterian church in America has in its membership 1,500 converted Jews, of whom sixty-one are ministers. In the Church of England there are over 300 clergy of the Jewish race . . . The Jewish Lexicon, published in Germany, estimates the number of Christian Jews who entered existing Christian churches, during the 19th century, at about 224,000." — Missionary Monthly — Reformed Review, Vol. 33, No. 396. How much surpassing Paul's day!

Do not now these Israelites mourn for him whom

---
1) cf. Rom. 11:25.
2) cf. Rom. 11:5.

they have pierced? Though there may be larger fulfillments to come, we should not ignore the incipient fulfillments even now visible.

Moreover, the percentage of Christian Jews is much greater than is generally imagined, in comparison with the percentage of Christian Gentiles. How few Gentiles are Christians, in comparison with the many that have never heard of the Christ, or have rejected him. And Jews have found such a welcome, in the Christian churches, that they are simply regarded as Christians.

For Christian Jews are considered Christians, rather than Jews, very frequently. Thus it becomes hardly recognized that there are thousands, and evidently hundreds of thousands of Jewish Christians, as indicated above.

Let us, therefore, not under-estimate the significance of Jewish Missions in the light of all the striking developments among the Jews of the nineteenth and twentieth centuries. As "the remnant (of Israel) according to the election of grace," (Rom. 11:5) is saved by becoming a part of the church of Christ, "the fulness of the Gentiles" (Rom. 11:25) is also saved by grace, in connection with the Church; "and so all Israel shall be saved," (Rom. 11:26), by grace, in connection with the church, when the Lord "shall take away their sins." (Rom. 11:27).

Even a widespread conversion of the Jews in many countries or a rather general conversion of the Palestinian Jews may become historical. Shall we not then say that the prophecies[1] were fulfilled in a very

---
1) cf. Rom. 11.

striking fashion, — more striking in fact than they themselves had required? In fact the Lord frequently does more than could be required of him, in connection with his promises or prophecies. For the Lord has revealed but little as to the future, on this score, and only history will fill the picture. The above kinds of literal fulfillments may not be necessary for our faith, but they may well cause the Premillenarian to pause.

In fact, the prophecies that refer to the Israel after the flesh are far less important than those referring to the spiritual Israel. For, apart from this spiritual Israel, the Israel after the flesh has no real future, though there may be an occasional prophecy having to do with the Israel, after the flesh.

Meanwhile the theocracy has come to a close with Jesus Christ. And the theocratic nation Israel has, therefore, no more today the same particularistic significance that it had in Old Testament days.

For Israel receives a spiritual significance to include Gentile believers as well as Jewish, as we have seen above.[1]

This, however, does not mean that the Israel after the flesh ceases to exist. Nor does it mean that the Israel after the flesh cannot become the object of God's prophecies. In fact, if Israel's return to Palestine is compared with prophecy, we may say that this present-day return would seem to be a literal fulfillment of prophecy if the prophecy may be thus literally interpreted.

---

[1] cf. Pages 100 and 150.

For, similarly, the prophecy, "Zion . . . shall be plowed, as a field," (Micah 3:12) does not apply spiritually to the church, but must be interpreted in some literal way, of the ancient locality of Zion. Moreover, the Israelitish people still "dwell alone" (Num. 23:9), as foretold by Balaam, and that not only in so far as Israel belongs spiritually to the church. Even in their opposition to the church, the Jews stand alone, as representative of the bitterest opposition.

Meanwhile, even a widespread conversion of the Jews would mean their accession to the church, and would, in no wise, carry with it the necessity of Christ reigning visibly on earth, in an earthly millennium.

For the scope of all the spiritual interpretations cited above points to Christ's spiritual kingship over his spiritual kingdom, the church.

Even with a Jewish return to Palestine and with the conversion of the Jews, Christ will be king of Jerusalem, of the promised land, and of Israel, as the king of his spiritual Zion and his spiritual Israel, his church, scattered throughout the world.[1]

5. *Unfulfilled Prophecies.*

But, now, as to the future, when it comes to unfulfilled prophecy, how then? Every student of the Scriptures knows that overweening confidence as to the precise manner in which a prophecy will be fulfilled is never in order. We know but in part. Sobriety of statement is required here.

We may very well derive caution from Jesus' words, spoken with reference to his first coming.

---

[1] For Abraham has become "heir of the world," Rom. 4:13, and not only heir of Canaan.

THE BIBLICAL SCOPE OF SPIRITUALIZATION 191

"From henceforth I tell you before it come to pass, that, when it is come to pass, ye may believe that I am *he*." — John 13:19.

From the manner in which prophecies were then fulfilled two things stand out prominently. There is a considerable scope of prophecies "fulfilled" literally. But there is also a definite scope of prophecies "fulfilled" spiritually. It was therefore necessary to devote a separate study to these fulfillments, to see how the Christ fulfilled the predictions concerning the prophetic, priestly and kingly tasks of his humiliation and of his exaltation, in so far as the completed steps of his exaltation have explicitly fulfilled the prophecies. In other words, we there saw how Christ became the king of his spiritual Zion, the church.

All the prophecies that concern the Messianic hope, thus come to stand out luminously, in their own Biblical perspective, for they show us, positively, how Christ would become king of Jerusalem, of the Promised Land, of Israel, by becoming king of the church.

And negatively, they create no apparent necessity for a more literal fulfillment, involving quite a different perspective, namely that of Premillennialism.

We thus see, on the one hand, that the Old Testament prophecies put forth no claim that requires their literal fulfillment within the thousand years of Revelation 20, as this chapter is interpreted by our Premillennial brethren. On the other hand, it also bears directly upon the study of the eschatological Old Testament prophecies, to see whether Rev. 20 in any way claims for itself the fulfillment of these prophecies, within the same thousand years, as this period is interpreted by Premillennialism. *Thus the study of Rev. 20 becomes a vital matter, for the study of the eschatology of the theocracy, a study that reinforces the above reached conclusions, when carried out in detail.*

6. *Conclusions.*

The scope of literally fulfilled prophecies and of the prophecies to be interpreted spiritually is therefore not only deducible from the Scriptural spiritualizations. But the results thus reached receive support both from Rev. 20 and especially from the fulfillments expressly cited in the New Testament.

Inferentially other O. T. eschatological passages than those explicitly fulfilled in the N. T. are to be interpreted according to the analogy of Scripture demonstrated above. On the basis of the New Testament fulfillments of Old Testament passages, dealing with the future of the kingdom, and on the basis of the interpretive principles, latent in the Old Testament and evident in the New, as they are manifested in the spiritualization of all the more important elements of the theocracy, we may discern, with gratitude, the intent of the Primary Author, the Holy Spirit, and explain such analogous prophecies as are not directly interpreted in the New Testament.

It would be an attractive task now to proceed with the exegesis of a number of other, individual passages to which the Premillenarians appeal. But to do lies outside of the scope of the present chapter.

Nevertheless, the direction in which that interpretation leads must certainly be in harmony with the rules of interpretation derived from the Old and New

Testament and with the New Testament interpretation of such passages as it quotes. And then the exegesis does not at all lead into the Premillenarian direction, but in the direction of our confessional standards, which hold that Christ will come to judge the quick and the dead.

Even with the light that the Scriptures give us concerning the future of the kingdom we shall often have to admit that we know but in part the exact force of certain prophecies, especially those that must still be fulfilled.

Concerning them we may apply the words which Jesus applies to prophecies of his First Coming, "And now I have told you before it come to pass, that, when it is come to pass, ye may believe." — John 14:29.

Meanwhile, we share with all Christians the fervent hope of His coming, and rejoice at the very thought of his appearing. With the entire Church of Jesus Christ, our prayer is, "Even so, Come quickly, Lord Jesus."

SUPPLEMENT

BIBLIOGRAPHICAL NOTE

The path of the reader, interested in the scope of the spiritualization of prophecy, has been made more attractive and easier, by the publication of a number of books.[1] For, though relatively few works treat this subject directly, many contribute to promote its study. These concern the character and content of prophecy, as well as its interpretation.

The prophecies, themselves, in so far as they have been adduced above, are quoted from the American Revised Version, used with satisfaction.

Here then follows an account of the works that have proved helpful, in the study of the future of the kingdom, in prophecy and fulfillment; and more particularly, the books found useful, in the study of the scope of spiritualization, as taught by Scripture, to illuminate prophecy; as well as the works indicating much of the scope of the literal fulfillments of prophecy.

These works may be grouped under three heads; and then concern, first, the nature of prophecy and its organic connection with sacred history; secondly, the general scope of spiritualization, — which is here a matter of primary importance; and thirdly, the related general scope of prophecies literally fulfilled.

I. CONCERNING THE NATURE OF PROPHECY AND ITS ORGANIC CONNECTION WITH SACRED HISTORY. (Cf. Chapters III–VI, inclusive.)

The organic connection of prophecy, in general, with its sacred historical background, is illustrated beautifully by Prof. Dr. J. Ridderbos, of the Kampen Seminary, Netherlands, in his work, "Het Godswoord der Profeten," which has been used by the writer, in part, for the present volume. (Instead of O. T. Sacred History, exclusively, Kampen Seminary

---

[1] The method of the above Bibliographical Note is derived, in a measure, from the illuminating Bibliographical Note, in the splendid work on John Calvin, by Prof. Williston Walker, of Yale. That this method is here followed, in part, is (of course not because Yale University brought the value of the writer's fellowships, etc., up to something over two thousand dollars, but) because Dr. Walker's method, in this regard, illustrates the best in use; and especially because a Bibliographical Note may indicate much better than merely a bibliography, how a work is related to prior studies concerned with a subject, and show, in brief, what research was involved, as well as the limited measure, in which a work aims to make a contribution. (Similarly, some university dissertations are required to contain a Bibliographical Note or a Critical, Bibliographical Discussion.)

offers Prophecy in its Historical Background, and its Interpretation, as treated in "Het Godswoord der Profeten."[1])

The real character of prophecy, as distinguished from soothsaying, is vindicated in an up-to-date fashion by Prof. Dr. G. Ch. Aalders, of the Free University of Amsterdam, in his remarkable study entitled, "De Profeten des Ouden Verbonds." The general principles of prophecy, there defended, are fundamental to the present study.

Much use has been made of the specialized works on Messianic Prophecy and O. T. Christology, by Franz Delitsch, Hengstenberg, Briggs, Huffmann, Stibitz, and Beecher.

Especially helpful were the thorough treatises of E. Riehm, collected in his "Messianic Prophecy," particularly that concerning "The Historical Character of Messianic Prophecy." Concerning this account, A. B. Davidson wrote, in the introduction to the English translation, "The organic connection of prophecy with history has been illustrated by Riehm with a wealth of examples exceeding anything hitherto done by others."

This work has been consulted especially in connection with Chapters IV–VI, though these Chapters, as well as the others, are worked up directly from the commentaries.

However, with respect to certain prophecies, especially concerning the *royal* character of the Servant of Jehovah in Isaiah, the present volume would aim to serve the reader with material derivative only, as far as we know, from the Old Testament.

Use of this material was, accordingly, made in a paper read before the American Oriental Society.

II. CONCERNING THE SCOPE OF SPIRITUALIZATION, IN PROPHECY AND IN ITS FULFILLMENT.
(Cf. Chapters VII–X, inclusive.)

This little work is devoted, especially, to the study of the scope, the sphere, of spiritualization, in Scripture. On this subject, the last word will not yet have been said for a long time. For it raises great differences of opinion, especially with the Premillenarians. Hence this field needs to be treated, increasingly, in an evidential fashion.

This work, then, aims to carry forward the Biblical investigation, at least in some measure. Grateful use was made of the evidence adduced in many works, especially those of Reformed writers.

Very important, among the works cited, is Principal Fair-

---

[1]) Incidentally, it was the writer's deeply appreciated privilege, to become acquainted with these Dutch scholars, in 1931; as well as other Biblical investigators, in his visiting the British Museum and the Louvre, Cambridge — especially Prof. Burkitt, The Free University of Amsterdam and Kampen; in hearing Professors Baer and Thilo lecture at Heidelberg and Bonn; and, especially, in studying the great repositories of archaelogy, art and history, in Egypt and Palestine, Beirut and Constantinople, Athens and Rome that illustrate Biblical revelation and history.

bairn's monumental "Typology of Scripture," and his subsequent work on "Prophecy," based on the "Typology."

Yet in his "Prophecy," he indicates that, in his own estimation, he has only laid the foundation, in proving the validity of the principles of spiritualization, and built a part of the superstructure in interpreting certain items of prophecy.[1]

In our Reformed theology, we are very much interested in the covenant of grace, and in the opposing view of the Premillenarians, that this covenant is among the things that have waxed aged, and have now vanished away, Hebrews 8:13.

In connection with this Premillennial position, it was found that especially the "new covenant," as contrasted with the old, Sinaitic covenant, and as founded upon the original, Abrahamic covenant, permitted of a more *exegetical* treatment, as against the Premillennialists, than was found in Fairbairn's works, or elsewhere; though our Reformed writers have treated the covenant of grace very broadly, in a *dogmatic* way.

In his work on Hermeneutics, Terry rejects the principle of spiritualization, summarily. On the other hand, this principle is accepted in the excellent and comprehensive manuals on Hermeneutics, of President L. Berkhof and of Prof. Dr. F. W. Grosheide, not to speak of other manuals. The former of these Reformed works gives some seven pages to the interpretation of prophecy. The latter work, being concerned with the New Testament, — "Hermeneutiek Ten Dienste van de Bestudeering van het Nieuwe Testament" — gives approximately a page to the question of the spiritualization of prophecy. Neither work takes up an itemized treatment of such terms as Zion, Israel, etc., nor the question of the scope of spiritualization.

The principle itself has been defended for centuries, as is clear from such works as Farrar's "History of Interpretation," and Diestel's "Geschichte des Alten Testamentes in der christlichen Kirche."

Since the scope of the principle of spiritualization, in Scripture, is not treated evidentially, in any hermeneutical study of our acquaintance, this seems to leave room for a contribution, in this field, particularly in connection with O. T. prophecy and its fulfillment; though Fairbairn and many others have done much work, of which one must make a grateful use, in the study of this subject.

Especially the present state of premillenarian discussion justifies the attempt to indicate, evidentially, and more completely, if possible, than was done heretofore, the sphere of spiritualization, in Scripture.

Particularly does it justify the accumulation of additional Biblical evidence, where available, for the spritualization of

---

1) Cf. Page V, of his "Prophecy."

Zion or Jerusalem, Israel and Edom, the inheritance of the once Holy Land, and many other greatly disputed points, touching the realm of spiritualization.

Use of this material was, accordingly, made in certain papers read before the Chicago Society of Biblical Research, and before some Ministers' Conferences.

III. CONCERNING THE RELATED GENERAL SCOPE OF PROPHECIES TO BE INTERPRETED LITERALLY OR LITERALLY FULFILLED. (Cf. Chapters I, II, the Survey at the beginning of Chapter III, and Chapter X.)

The scope of spiritualization, and its applicability, also tend to establish the line of demarcation of prophecies to be interpreted literally, as discussed in Chapter X.

A survey of prophecies literally fulfilled, in the course of history, is given at the opening of Chapter III. This survey is based chiefly on Urquhart's "Wonders of Prophecy," which appears to be quite neutral, with respect to the question of premillennialism. It quotes many standard historical works. This survey is also based on Davis' "Prophecies That Prove the Bible," and "Keith's "Letterlijke Vervulling." The latter work also seems to show no bias in favor of premillennialism.

Items on Zionism were taken from the above mentioned work of Davis, as well as from Prof. R. B. Kuiper's "While the Bridegroom Tarries." Some magazine articles on the subject were also considered.

The very partial return of the Jews to Palestine, in modern times, cannot be used consistently, in favor of premillennialism, by the adherents of the Scofield Bible; though some other premillenarians seems to see a support for their position in these events.

In view of this latter fact, some attention was given to this theme in Chapter X, and especially to do full justice to all that may be involved here.

But it is found that, even if one should see a literal fulfillment of prophecy, in these events, this does not yield any support to the positions of the premillennialists.

Meanwhile, the spiritual significance of the Jews now in Palestine cannot be well understood, until history has proceeded to disclose it. In any case, it concerns, chiefly, the remnant of Israel, according to the election of grace, whether larger or smaller.

But this question is considered to be of far less importance than the positive evidence for the spiritualization of prophecy and for its scope.

No one is more aware of the shortcomings of this volume than the writer. Meanwhile, he aims to continue the investigation, and will appreciate receiving copies of reviews of his little book.

May the Lord's indispensable blessing rest upon it, to the glory of His Name and the welfare of His Church.

INDEX OF TOPICS

Touching the Scope of Spiritualization and the Scope of Literally Fulfilled Prophecies

	PAGE
Abrahamic covenant	131
Abraham, seed of, spiritually interpreted	97
Application of Biblical principles of interpretation	175, 178
Ark spiritually interpreted	113
Biblical principles of interpretation	143
Bride of the Lord as the covenant people	98
Canaan spiritually interpreted	91, 147
Candlestick spiritually interpreted	120
Character of kingdom spiritualized	28, 142, 174
Church and the kingdom	94, 118, 143, 166, 174, 176
Circumcision spiritually interpreted	132, 134
Circumcision spiritually interpreted as baptism	132
Conclusions	192
Conquest of enemies spiritually interpreted	111, 112
Covenant, Abrahamic	131
Covenant, new	127
Covenant, old	121, 122, 127
Criticism of premillennial principles of interpretation	73
Davidic throne spirtually interpreted	159
Denial of spiritualization	23
Edomites spiritually interpreted	108, 168
Eschatology	13
Eschatology of the theocracy	35, 37, 47, 57
Future of the kingdom	35, 37, 47, 57
Gog	181, 182
Holy land spiritually interpreted	91, 147
How apply scope of spiritualization in interpreting prophecy	175, 178
Import of premillennial principles of interpretation	71
Individual prophecies, how interpreted	175
Israel spiritually interpreted	100, 150
Israel's return to Palestine	181–190
Jerusalem spiritually interpreted	88, 144, 178
Jewish return to Palestine	181–190
Kingdom and the church	94, 118, 143, 166, 174, 176
Kingdom, future of	35, 37, 47, 57
Kingdom spiritually interpreted	94, 174

INDEX OF TOPICS

	PAGE
Literally fulfilled prophecies surveyed	26, 179, 182

Millennial, see premillennial

New covenant	127
Old covenant	121, 126–130
Old covenant spiritually interpreted	121, 122, 127
Old Testament Scriptures organically spiritualized	140
Organic spiritualization	135
Palestine spiritually interpreted	91, 147
Passover spiritually interpreted	135
Premillennial view concerning Christ's royal office	79
Premillennial view concerning Jesus' priestly activities	76
Premillennial view concerning our Lord's prophetic work	75
Premillennial interpretation of prophecy	70
Priestly and sacrificial types of Christ and of his church	57
Priestly types of the church, spiritually interpreted	116
Priestly types of Christ, spiritually interpreted	164
Principles of interpretation, Biblical	143
Principles of interpretation, Premillennial	70
Promised land, spiritually interpreted	91, 147
Prophecies, how interpreted	175
Prophetic types of Christ and of his church	37
Prophetic types of the church, spiritually interpreted	119
Prophetic types of Christ, spiritually interpreted	162
Psalter organically spiritualized	136
Royal types of Christ and of his church	47
Royal types of the church, spiritually interpreted	118
Royal types of Christ, spiritually interpreted	166
Sacraments spirtually interpreted	134
Sacrifices spiritually interpreted	114
Scope of prophecies interpreted literally	26, 179
Scope of spiritualization in Scripture	143, 174
Seed of Abraham spiritually interpreted	97
Spiritual interpretation defined	84
Spiritualization defined	84
Survey of literally fulfilled prophecies	26, 173
Survey of scope of spiritualization in Scripture	143, 174
Temple spiritually interpreted	113
Theocracy	28, 142, 174
Theocracy, eschatology of	35, 37, 47, 57
Throne of David, spiritually interpreted	159
Unfulfilled prophecies	190
Zion spiritually interpreted	88, 144
Zionism	182–190

INDEX OF SCRIPTURE REFERENCES

GENESIS

CHAPTER	PAGE
12:3	74
15:6	131
15:18	133
17:7	131–132
22:16	133
49:10	36, 172

EXODUS

2:24	134
6:4–8	134
12:40	124
12:48–50	100, 105
15:18	28, 133
19	29, 59, 94
19:4–9	29
19:5	98
19:5, 6	29, 94, 121
19:6	26, 27, 116, 117, 118, 121
20	30
22	31
24:6–8	125, 127
32:34	40

LEVITICUS

10:8–11	31
26:30–33	26, 180
26:30–36	26, 114

NUMBERS

11:29	45
18:20	91
23:9	185, 190

DEUTERONOMY

7:9	-134
8:18	134
9:5	134
10:15	134
10:16	134
17:15–18	32
17:18	35
18:2	91

CHAPTER	PAGE
18:14, 15	32
18:15	38, 39, 162, 163
23:8	109
29:22	26, 180
30:6	134
31:9–11	31
33:4, 5	28

JOSHUA

5:14, 15	40
6:2	40

JUDGES

2:1–5	40
5:4, 5	109
6:11–14	40

I SAMUEL

15:22	114

II SAMUEL

7:13	38, 167
7:13–16	154, 155
7:16	47, 83

I KINGS

16:30	19

II KINGS

25:10	21

I CHRONICLES

6:4–15	78

EZRA

1:7–10	51, 76
3:2	65, 76, 78
3:4	67
10:10	185

NEHEMIAH

2:2	185
4:7	186
12:1, 8	78
13:15	185

PSALMS

2:8	94
12:16	24
16:5	91, 137
16:10	138, 139
19:8	24

Index of Scripture References

CHAPTER	PAGE
22:1	137, 138
22:18	137
27:6	63
40:7–10	42, 43
45:5	63
51:17	63, 114, 137
54:6	63
68:18	138, 139
69:9	43
72	48
73:26	91, 137
74:12	94, 95
107:22	114, 137
110	57, 138, 139, 165, 170
110:1	170, 171
110:5	165
118:22	137, 138
119:57	91, 137
122:6	27, 90
141:2	62, 114, 137
142:5	91, 137

ISAIAH

1:9, 10	103
1:27	66
2:2, 3	66, 73
4:2	53, 54
6:1	49
8:11, 12	26, 180
9	169, 172
9:6	161
9:7	83, 154
11:1, 14	53, 54, 72, 74, 79
13:19–22	26
14:23	26
19	94
19:21–25	63, 102, 114
19:25	94, 151
24:5	108
34:10, 11	26
41:21, 22	13
42:1–4	164
42:3	119
42:1–6	52, 53
42:6	119
42:5–16	74
42:6	44
42—53	54
43:1	151
43:10	52, 53, 119, 155

Chapter	Page
43:15	94, 95
44:5	105, 152
44:21	151
44—45	51, 52, 101
45:22–25	104
47:1	26
49:6	44
49:14	88, 144
50:1, 4	99
50:6	44
51:2	89
51:3	88, 89, 144
51:17	89
51:23	89
52:1	144
52:1, 2	89
52:1–11	51
52:11–13	50, 58
52:12	155, 156
52:13	49, 155
52:13–53	155, 156
52:15	156
53:2	53
53:3	167
53:6	54
53:7	164
53:10	58, 76, 155
53:10–13	58
53:12	49, 50, 51, 55, 155
54:2	150
54:3	150
54:5	150
55:3, 4	38, 52, 53
55:3	155
55:4	150
56:3	103, 105
58:8, 10	119
60:1	119
61	44, 45
63:1, 3	109
66:20, 21	59, 63, 74, 78

JEREMIAH

Chapter	Page
2:2	29
3:16	63, 113
4:4	134
6:10	134
9:26	134
10:16	91, 134
23:5	53, 54, 55

CHAPTER	PAGE
30:6	134
30:21	58
31:31–34	107, 122, 123, 125, 127, 129, 130, 131
33:11	64
33:15	53, 54
33:17	60, 117
33:18	60, 64, 117
47:5	26
49:2	26
49:6	26, 180
49:16	26
50:10–26	26
51:19	91
51:25–36	26

EZEKIEL

16:60	29
21:27	36, 56
25:3, 4	26
25:11	26
26:3, 4, 5, 12, 14	14
26:12	179
28:22, 23	17
29:15	26
30:4–16	26
35:3–9	26
36:33–35	26, 180
36:33–38	180
38:8	181
40—47	113
40—48	72, 76, 113, 165, 166
42:13	46, 76
43:13	76
43:13, 19	73
43:19	65, 76, 78
43:26	65
43:20, 22	65, 73
43:20, 26	65, 73, 76
43:26	73
44:1	77
44:9–11	66
44:10	61
44:9–15	117
44:15	61
45:17	65, 66, 73, 76, 117
47	67, 77
47:1	165
47:10	165
47:1–10	165

DANIEL

CHAPTER	PAGE
7	172
7:13, 14	41, 56, 172
9:26	55

HOSEA

2	98
6:6	114
14:2	62, 114

JOEL

2:28, 29	46, 119

AMOS

1:2	181
3:14, 15	26
9	110, 168
9:7, 8	102
9:11	48, 112
9:11, 12	152, 168
9:11–12	110, 111
9:12	109, 151

OBADIAH

1:15	108

MICAH

1:6	19, 179
3:12	20, 179, 190
5:1	167
6:5–8	63

HABAKKUK

3:2, 3, 5	109

ZEPHANIAH

2:1–6	26
2:4	26
3:15	74
9:5	26

ZECHARIAH

3	54, 58
3:8	53, 54, 76, 164
3:8, 9	59
4:1–6	120
4:6	76
6	54, 58, 59
6:12, 13	54
6:13	38
9:5	26

Index of Scripture References

CHAPTER	PAGE
9:9	156, 170, 179
14	72, 73
16:16	67, 68
14:16, 20, 21	65
14:21	68

MALACHI

1:6	62, 69
1:11	68, 74, 117
2:1, 8	62
2:3, 6	62
2:4	62
2:4, 5	62, 117
2:5	62
3:1	40
3:3	62

MATTHEW

2:6	167
4:13	169
4:19	165
5:5	92, 93, 133, 147
8:11	95, 96
9:15	99, 154
12:7–21	164
16:18, 19	157, 158, 161
21:4, 5	170
21:5	147
21:42	138
21:43	95
22:44	139
25:33	79
26:26–28	135
26:64	172
27:35	139
27:46	139

MARK

12:10	138
12:36	139
14:12–15	135
15:18	139
15:34	139

LUKE

2:32	74
10:17	138
11:50, 51	163
12:35	120
16:24	77

CHAPTER	PAGE
19:33	43
20:42	139
22:7–20	135
22:20	125, 127
23:24	139
24:19	163

JOHN

1:45	162
2:17	43
3:29, 30	99, 154
4:6	77
4:10	77, 165
4:13	77
4:14	77
4:20–24	114
4:45	163
5:27–29	166
5:46	162
6:14	163
7:37	77
12:13	156, 179
12:41	49
13:19	191
14:29	193
18:36	97
19:24	139

ACTS

2:16–18	121
2:29–36	160
2:30	41, 139
2:33	83
2:34	139
2:34–36	170, 171
2:39	131
3:22	163
4:11	138
5:31	171
7:37	163
8:32, 33	49
8:32–35	164, 165
13:35	139
13:47	74
15:13–18	111
15:16–18	168
15:17	109, 110, 151, 152
15:18	168
26:18	74

INDEX OF SCRIPTURE REFERENCES

ROMANS

CHAPTER	PAGE
2:28, 29	134, 135
4:12	97
4:13	92, 93, 133, 147, 148, 150, 190
7:4	91, 99
8	25
9	24, 25, 98
9:6	106
9:27	97
11	24, 25, 187, 188
11:5	187, 188
11:16	151
11:17	106
11:17–24	127, 156
11:19	151, 154, 156
11:24	151, 154, 156
11:25	187, 188
11:26	154, 156, 188
11:27	188
13	13, 29, 30
14:17	96
15:8	135

I CORINTHIANS

5:7	114, 135, 144
6:9	134
7:14	132
11:25	125, 127
12:13	105
12:27	105
12:28	105
15:25	171
15:50	134

II CORINTHIANS

2:17	128
2:3	130
3:3	127
3:6	124, 127, 130
3:7	127
5:21	76
6:16	77, 113
11:2	91, 99

GALATIANS

1:4	49
3:6–17	131
3:15–17	126, 131
3:17	124
3:29	27, 92, 93, 97, 148, 150
4:26	90, 145

EPHESIANS

CHAPTER	PAGE
1:20	171
1:22	171
2:12	95, 96, 105, 107, 127, 153, 154
2:14	105
2:19	96, 107, 127, 153
4:8	139
5:5	134
5:23–33	91, 99

PHILIPPIANS

2:14, 15	120
3:3	135

COLOSSIANS

1:13	88, 95, 107, 153, 157, 158, 161
2:11, 12	132, 135
3:1	171
3:11	105, 135
3:24	92, 93

I TIMOTHY

2:5	49

TITUS

2:14	49
3:7	134

HEBREWS

1:3	171
1:13	139
5:6, 10	165
6:1	132
6:2	132
6:13–17	133
6:17, 18	133
6:20	165
7:15	165
7:17	165
8	130
8:1	171
8:3	127, 164
8:8	123
8:9	123, 127
8:8–12	123
8:10	107, 125, 127, 132, 133
8:12	131
8:13	123, 124, 126, 130
9	113
9:2	77
9:15	92, 93, 134, 148

CHAPTER	PAGE
9:19, 20	125, 127
9:28	49
10:7	42
10:10	165
10:12	171
10:18	127
11:8	134
11:10	91, 93
12:12	144
12:22	90
12:23	107
13:14, 15, 16	114

I PETER

1:3	93, 149
1:4	93, 133
1:4, 5	133
1:18	93
1:19	93
1:24	93
2:4	114, 117
2:5	77, 113, 114
2:7	138
2:9	26, 117, 118, 160
2:10	160

REVELATION

1:4	117
1:6	117
1:20	120
2:9	106
3:12	90
3:21	118
5:9, 10	118
19:7, 8	154
20	80, 191, 192
20:8	181
21	106
21:1	77, 154
21:1–3	114
21:9	90, 91, 145
21:9–12	99, 106, 127, 154, 157
21:9, 12	127
21:10	145
22:1	77, 161, 165
22:1–5	114
22:5	119
22:14	118
22:16	119

www.ingramcontent.com/pod-product-compliance
Lightning Source LLC
Chambersburg PA
CBHW050147170426
43197CB00011B/2001